"The Gift Beyond Compare!"

Thirty-Three Reflections on the Holy Eucharist As Sacrifice and Sacrament

Text

Father Richard J. Rego, S.T. L.
Priest of the Diocese of Tucson, Arizona

Cover

Father Gene Plaisted, O.S.C.

Nihil Obstat: Richard J. Schuler
Censor Deputatus

Imprimatur: ✠ Harry J. Flynn, D.D.
Archbishop of St. Paul and Minneapolis

The Leaflet Missal Company

976 W. Minnehaha Ave.   St. Paul, Minnesota 55104

Printed in U.S.A.
ISBN 1-885845-26-X

"THE GIFT BEYOND COMPARE!"

THIRTY-THREE REFLECTIONS ON THE HOLY EUCHARIST AS SACRIFICE AND SACRAMENT

DEDICATION

In a spirit of filial love and devotion, I dedicate these thirty-three reflections to the Ever Virgin Mother of God and Our Blessed Mother. Most Holy Mother, teach us to love Jesus in the Most Blessed Sacrament of the Altar. Just as you "stood by the Cross" on Calvary, stand by us when we assist at the Holy Sacrifice of the Mass. Teach us to love the Eucharistic Sacrifice, for the Mass is Calvary.

Dearest mother in heaven, teach us to love Our Lord Jesus in the Blessed Sacrament. By your humble "Fiat" at the Annunciation, you conceived by the power of the Holy Spirit. The Second Person of the Blessed Trinity became Flesh of your flesh, Bone of your bone. From that instant, you loved Our Lord Jesus with a love beyond all telling. Teach us to have some small measure of your devotion when we receive Him in Holy Communion.

Holy Mother, hear our prayers of reparation for all who have lost faith and respect for His Eucharistic Presence. We beseech you to bring the Church of our days to a renewed awareness of that "Gift Beyond Compare," Jesus in the Most Holy Sacrament of the Altar. We place our confidence in you, for you are Our Lady of the Most Blessed Sacrament.

FOREWORD

On the occasion of the 30th anniversary of the Decree *Presbyterorum Ordinis* of the Second Vatican Council, the Roman Congregation of the Clergy organized, on October 27, 1995, a symposium commemorating this event. Broadcast throughout the whole world, it culminated in a recital with worldwide representation and participation. The Holy Father took part personally in the performance.

In his closing address, the Holy Father gave a profound testimony of his own priesthood. It was a moving witness of the Priesthood of the Catholic Church. Offering daily Mass, he said, is absolutely the center of his life and of his daily activities. It is also the central point of the theology of the priesthood.

Undoubtedly, we can add that the Holy Sacrifice of the Mass and the Blessed Sacrament are the uncontested center of the life of every Catholic. In this period of our earthly decision for eternal life, the Holy Eucharist is the pledge to reach our heavenly goal which is participation in the glory of God in eternal life.

Consequently, today's crisis of belief in the Eucharist and the crisis of life of the faithful, provides ample evidence of a serious situation. It is a crisis of faith and Catholic life in the whole Church.

At the heart of this crisis is quite naturally the Catholic priesthood. The identity of the Priesthood is principally defined by the Holy Sacrifice of the Mass and faithfulness to the Blessed Eucharist. Whenever the priest is no longer convinced of his own identity and of his mission, he can no longer communicate the Eucharistic faith and life to the faithful. Instead, he will transfer to them his own weakness and infidelity. Moreover, whenever the higher superiors in the Church, who have responsibility in doctrine and government, no longer care about this central point of their pastoral duties or they themselves hesitate in their Eucharistic faith and convictions, they must consider Christ's challenge to His Apostles on the shore of Lake Genesareth as being addressed to them directly. Confronted with the difficulties of many of his disciples to believe in the mystery of the Eucharist, Our Lord told His Apostles openly: And you, would you also like to leave (me)?

Father Richard J. Rego, well aware of today's situation among priests and, consequently, also among many faithful, has decided to offer Catholics a series of 33 Eucharistic Reflections. His purpose, as he explicitly states, is to remind the faithful of the Church's doctrine concerning the nature of the Holy Sacrifice of the Mass and the Real Presence of Christ in the Blessed Sacrament with His divinity and humanity, soul and body, flesh and blood. Father Rego does this in a clear manner, strengthening the Catholic consciousness of the Eucharist as sacrifice and sacrament.

In these 33 meditations, Father Rego tries to vivify and to deepen the conviction of this great mystery, which is the object of our Eucharistic faith. He also strives to illuminate the relation of this sacrament to the faithful and also the particular connection between the Eucharist and the priest as *alter Christus* in his proper office as minister of this sacrament.

Father Rego, moreover, explains the relation between Christ in the Eucharist and His holy mother, the instrument whom God has elected in order to realize His design of salvation. He further explains the relation among all the other saints and even between every Catholic who unites his sacrifice with the Sacrifice of Christ on the Cross.

In his meditations, the author focuses at length on various kinds of public devotions, both liturgical and extra-liturgical expressions. He thoroughly instructs the faithful so that they can better understand and increasingly use these precious pearls of Eucharistic worship and other expressions of Catholic piety.

Concerning the lack of proper behavior in front of the Blessed Eucharist, which today often is apparent among Catholics, the Council of Trent has already pointed out that the lack of awe corresponds to a lack of piety and even more: a positive irreverence corresponds to a real impiety.

But I want to emphasize in these meditations Father Rego's clear purpose, namely to stimulate a positive deepening of Eucharistic faith and piety rather than to denounce polemically the errors in this central field of Catholic faith. In these 33 meditations, these distortions are implicitly corrected.

In this time of serious crisis of faith in the Church, these reflections can be a joyful consolation and a great help for priests insofar as they are the representatives of Christ in offering the Sacrifice of the Mass and in administrating the sacraments. Indeed, this same consolation and joy extends to all Catholics insofar as the promise of Our Lord concerns them today more than in other times: "Whoever eats my Flesh and drinks my Blood has eternal life and I will raise him on the last day" (John 6: 54).

Alfons M. Cardinal Stickler

INTRODUCTION

An anguished hush settled on the Sunday morning congregation. From the pulpit, the priest held a Host in his hand. He lifted the Sacred Species high over his head and said: "This is bread, plain and simple! It is nothing else! It is not the Body of Christ!"

This incident did not take place during the Reformation. The priest was neither Martin Luther, who denied the Mass as the Sacrifice of Calvary made present, nor Thomas Cranmer, who denied both the Mass as Sacrifice and the Real Presence of Our Lord in the Eucharist. No! These appalling words came from a Catholic priest who is the pastor of a large parish in the United States. Sadly, he is alone neither in his disbelief nor in his ardor to proclaim it.

My purpose in presenting these Eucharistic reflections to you is not to dwell on such dreadful desecrations. It is to confirm our faith in two core dogmas which are at the heart of Catholicism: 1) The Holy Sacrifice of the Mass is one with and identical to the Sacrifice that Our Blessed Lord offered on the Cross of Calvary. On Calvary, Jesus Christ offered Himself up to the Heavenly Father in a bloody manner. At every Mass, the priest, acting in the Person of Jesus Christ, offers to the Father the same, identical Sacrifice in an unbloody manner (see Sacred Council of Trent, Session 22). The *Catechism of the Catholic Church* teaches: "The Sacrifice of Christ and the Sacrifice of the Eucharist are one single Sacrifice" (N. 1367). 2) Jesus Christ is *really, truly* and *substantially* present in the Blessed Sacrament. He is present *Body, Blood, Soul* and *Divinity* (see *Catechism,* N. 1374). When the priest says the words of consecration at the Holy Sacrifice of the Mass, a *transubstantiation* takes place (see *Catechism,* N. 1376). In that instant, bread ceases to be bread. Wine ceases to be

1

wine. They become the Body and Blood of Our Divine Lord and Savior, Jesus Christ. The presence of Christ is not symbolic, as some have insisted throughout the centuries. It is His *"Real Presence!"*

My fervent prayer is that these 33 Eucharistic meditations will draw us to a deeper understanding of the Church's teachings. May Mary, Our Lady of the Most Blessed Sacrament, lead us to an enduring and intense love for the Eucharist as Sacrifice and Sacrament. May St. Joseph, the Foster Father of Our Lord and the Universal Patron of the Church, accompany us on our Eucharistic journey as he always accompanied Jesus and Mary.

O Sacrament Most Holy, O Sacrament Divine, all praise and all thanksgiving be every moment Thine. Amen!

Fr. Richard J. Rego
Immaculate Conception Church
Ajo, Arizona
Feast of Corpus Christi, 1996

"TASTE AND SEE THE GOODNESS OF THE LORD!"

Often in Masses with a Eucharistic theme, the Church prays the 34th Psalm, "Taste and see the goodness of the Lord." Literally, in the Holy Eucharist, we do precisely this. We taste and see the goodness of the Lord. Our goal in these reflections is to increase our knowledge, devotion and love for the Holy Eucharist as Sacrifice and Sacrament.

How well I remember my altar-boy days at the Annunciation Parish in Philadelphia. The reverence of the priests for the Blessed Sacrament was striking. I recall the processions with long lines of altar boys. As Father carried the Blessed Sacrament under the canopy, girls dressed in white paved the church's aisles with flower petals. Strains of the *Pange Lingua Gloriosi* seemed to descend from the very heavens. "May I become a priest," I prayed. No doubt Our Eucharistic Lord was sowing the seeds of vocations. Four of us altar boys later became priests.

Private Devotions

Aside from public devotions we should develop our personal, private Eucharistic devotions. Especially helpful are spiritual readings on the Blessed Eucharist. Weekly, or at least monthly, Confession does much to increase our Eucharistic devotion. Frequent visits to the Blessed Sacrament are especially important. Praying the Rosary during these visits places us under the special care of Our Blessed Mother, who always teaches us about Jesus.

The "hidden Jesus," as the Fatima children called Him, awaits us in the tabernacle; no appointment is necessary. The longer one stays in His Presence, the more pleased He is with us. I know a layman who spent at least two hours daily before the tabernacle. When I asked him what he said to the Lord, he responded: "Not much. Mostly,

3

I just look at Him and He looks at me. Don't good friends do that at times?" Jesus, our divine Friend, silently awaits us in the tabernacle. He wants to be with us and we want to be with Him.

Daily Mass And Communion

The most effective way to grow in love for the Eucharistic Lord is the practice of daily Mass and Communion. The *Catechism of the Catholic Church* teaches: "The Church strongly encourages the faithful to receive the Holy Eucharist on Sundays and feast days, or more often still, even daily" (N. 1389). Did not Our Lord say: "He who eats my Flesh and drinks my Blood lives in Me and I in him" (John 6: 56)?

May these reflections lead us to a greater love for our Eucharistic Lord. Jesus loves us with an infinite love. If anyone doubts His Love, gaze upon the Crucified Savior. Jesus, on the Cross of Calvary, proves His love with the last drop of His Blood. In the Blessed Sacrament, Jesus awaits us with an ocean of love, an abundance of graces and a joy which He alone can give. Whatever love we give Him, He returns a hundredfold.

Yet, I fear that on the Day of Judgment all of us will share one huge regret. It will be that, during our earthly lives, we were not aflame with love for the Eucharistic Lord. The great saint of the Eucharist, St. Peter Eymard, wrote: "Ah! How fearful we will be on the Day of Judgment for having lived with so much love at our side and paid no heed to it" (*The Real Presence,* p.111).

May the Holy Mother of God and Our Blessed Mother, inspire us to love Our Lord Jesus in the Blessed Sacrament more and more!

"LET A MAN EXAMINE HIMSELF!"

"We are Ambassadors for Christ, God making His appeal to you through us. We beseech you on behalf of Christ, be reconciled to God" (2 Corinthians 5:20). In every age, the Church echoes this fervent appeal of St. Paul. Reflecting on the Eucharist, let us heed the great Apostle's exhortation. Prompted by the Holy Spirit, he exhorts us to cleanse our souls in the Sacrament of Penance. When we receive Holy Communion we want to be as prepared as possible. We want to be free from every stain of sin.

Frequent Holy Communion

Our Divine Savior's words are unmistakable: "Unless you eat the Flesh of the Son of Man and drink His Blood, you will not have life in you" (John 6:53). The Church has always understood the Lord's mandate in the sense of frequent Communion. Centuries ago, the Council of Trent urged the faithful attending Mass to receive Holy Communion (Session XXII, chapter VI). Today, the *Catechism of the Catholic Church* invites Catholics to receive every Sunday and Holy Day, even *daily* (N. 1389). If one were to receive only once a year, as canon law requires (Canon 920), one truly would be dying spiritually. If the body cannot survive without food, how much more catastrophic is spiritual starvation?

One Must Be Free From Mortal Sin

From apostolic times the Church has been clear that a person must be in the state of sanctifying grace before receiving the Eucharist. The Catechism says: "To respond to this invitation we must *prepare ourselves* for so great and so holy a moment. St. Paul urges us to examine our conscience: 'Whoever, therefore, eats the bread and drinks the cup of the Lord in an unworthy manner will be guilty of profaning the body and blood of the Lord. Let a man examine himself, and so eat of the body and drink of the cup. For anyone who eats and drinks without discerning the body eats and drinks judgment upon himself' (1 Corinthians 11:27-29). Therefore, anyone conscious of grave sin must receive the Sacrament of Penance before going to Communion" (N. 1385).

Reiterating the teachings of Trent, the Catechism reminds us that "even if he feels deep contrition," one must not receive without prior Confession (see N. 1457). However, some have been deluded into believing that an act of contrition before Communion suffices when one is in mortal sin. This is not true. Ordinarily, one who is in mortal sin must make a sacramental confession before receiving Holy Communion (*Code of Canon Law,* N. 916).

Bishop Robert Carlson of Sioux Falls in his Pastoral Letter, The Pledge of Future Glory, June 18, 1995, teaches: "When conscious of any mortal sin, a person is obliged to confess all sins to a priest within the Sacrament of Penance before approaching the Altar to receive Holy Communion. To receive Holy Communion unworthily is to commit a sacrilege: 'a grave sin especially when committed against the Eucharist (*Catechism of the Catholic Church,* N. 2120).'"

Eucharistic Fast

Catholic piety requires that we prepare for the reception of the Eucharist by fasting. Years ago, the fast began at midnight and lasted until one received. This law now has been relaxed greatly. "Whoever is to receive the Blessed Sacrament is to abstain for at least one hour before Holy Communion from all food and drink, with the sole exception of water and medicine . . . The elderly and those who are suffering from some illness, also those who care for them, may receive the Blessed Sacrament even if within the preceding hour they have consumed something" (Canon N. 920).

Because of our need for the Eucharist, the Church, in its pastoral concern for souls, does not wish to make these requirements overly burdensome. Yet, the Lord Jesus wants us to be obedient to His Church. Everything the Church does is done in view of her mission, the salvation of souls. Thus, the Eucharistic fast cannot be taken lightly.

One Must Be Catholic

The Holy Eucharist is also the "sign of unity" among Christ's faithful. It reveals our solidarity in faith, morals and liturgy. Therefore, Church law mandates that only Catholics can receive the Eucharist (see Canon N. 844). Non-Catholics are most welcome to join us in prayer. The Catholic Church longs for Christian unity. May we join in Jesus' prayer at the Last Supper that "all may be one as you, Father, are in me and I in you and that they may be one in us" (John 17:21).

Having observed these fundamental requirements, let us approach the "altar of God" with confidence. Our Beloved Savior did not merely invite us to receive Him. He issued a divine command: "Unless you eat my Body and drink my Blood, you will have no life in you!" Is there a more intimate union possible than the Holy Eucharist? Jesus wants to be united with us! He wants us to be united with Him, always. The Blessed Eucharist is the outpouring of our Lord's infinite love for every man and woman. St. Ignatius of Antioch said: "For my drink, I crave the Blood of Christ, which is love imperishable." Our Blessed Lord is really, truly and substantially the Bread of Life.

Mindful of our complete unworthiness, let us humbly repeat the centurion's prayer as we approach the Blessed Eucharist: "Lord, I am not worthy that Thou should come under my roof. Yet, only say the word and my soul shall be healed" (Matthew 8:8).

"THE CHRIST WHO CALLS US TO THE EUCHARIST, CALLS US TO PENANCE!"

In his book *Holy Communion,* St. Peter Julian Eymard writes: "Let us bear in mind that the preparation for Communion that Jesus desires most to see in us is that of Mary when she said, 'Behold the handmaid of the Lord'" (p. 24). Our Blessed Mother, who was immaculately conceived, never committed even the slightest venial sin. God found in her a "worthy" mother to receive His Son. In imitation of Our Lady, people who believe in the Eucharist endeavor to live a holy life by avoiding all sin, both mortal and venial.

Clearly venial sins should never prevent us from receiving Holy Communion. We have a divine mandate from Our Lord to eat His Body and drink His Blood (see John 6). Nevertheless, we should strive to receive Holy Communion as worthily as possible. Our Lord said: "Be perfect as your Heavenly Father is perfect" (Matthew 5:48).

The *Catechism of the Catholic Church* teaches that: "Venial sin weakens charity; it manifests a disordered affection for created goods; it impedes the soul's progress in the exercise and the practice of moral good; it merits temporal punishment. Deliberate and unrepented venial sins disposes us little by little to commit mortal sin." Quoting St. Augustine, it states: "While in the flesh, man cannot help but have at least some light sins. But do not trivialize these sins which we call "light": if you take them for light when you weigh them, tremble when you count them. A number of light objects makes a great mass; a number of drops fills a river; a number of grains makes a heap. What then is our hope? Above all, confession . . . " (N. 1863).

The Eucharist And Penance

In his encyclical letter, *The Redeemer of Man,* Pope

John Paul II teaches: "The Eucharist and Penance become, in a sense, two closely connected dimensions of authentic life in accordance with the spirit of the Gospel and a truly Christian life. The Christ who calls us to the Eucharistic Banquet is always the same Christ who exhorts us to penance and repeats His "repent" (Mark 1:15). Without this constant ever renewed endeavor for conversion, partaking in the Eucharist would lack its full redeeming effectiveness" (N. 20).

The Holy Father is emphatic that the frequent reception of Holy Communion should lead us to make more frequent confessions. The devout reception of the Eucharist makes us aware of our unworthiness. We want to be cleansed of every stain of sin and become as pure as possible. These holy sentiments direct us to the Sacrament of Penance. Confession, conversely, makes us aware of our total helplessness apart from God's grace. Jesus said: "Without me, you can do nothing" (John 15:5). The Sacrament of Penance, in turn, points us to the Holy Eucharist where we receive grace in abundance to overcome our sins. One sacrament leads to the other. As we strive to grow in love for the Eucharistic Lord, let us seriously examine our confessional habits.

Pope John Paul II also teaches that the faithful should receive the sacrament with "reasonable frequency." What is "reasonable frequency?" Weekly confession is always the ideal. From time immemorial, spiritual directors and confessors have recommended the pious practice of weekly confession.

St. Francis deSales consistently instructed those under his spiritual direction: "Go to confession every week, humbly and devoutly, even though you may not have any mortal sins on your conscience . . . The Sacrament of Confession not only absolves venial sins but also strengthens you to avoid falling into the same sins again. It enlightens you to recognize your sins more clearly and repairs the damage they may have caused" (*Introduction to the Devout Life,* Chapter 19).

Weekly confession is important, not only for priests and religious, but for all members of Christ's Mystical Body. If this is not possible or convenient, monthly confession should be the minimum standard. This is a key message of the Nine First Friday and the Five First Saturday Devotions. Devout families set aside time each month for confession. It is truly edifying when Mom, Dad and the children line up to make their individual confessions. No doubt the Lord Jesus showers the family with innumerable blessings. Everyone - - popes, cardinals, bishops, priests, sisters and laity - - is a sinner who is in need of penance. St. John says: "If we say, 'we are free of the guilt of sin, we deceive ourselves; the truth is not to be found in us'" (1 John 1:8).

"By The Inspiration Of The Holy Spirit"

Pope Pius XII taught: "It is true that venial sins may be expiated in many ways which are to be highly recommended. But to insure more rapid progress day by day in the path of virtue, We will that the pious practice of frequent confession, which was introduced into the Church by the inspiration of the Holy Spirit, should be earnestly advocated. By it, genuine self-knowledge is increased, Christian humility grows, bad habits are corrected, spiritual neglect and tepidity are resisted, the conscience is purified, the will is strengthened, a salutary self-control is attained, and grace is increased in virtue of the sacrament itself. Let those among the younger clergy who make light of or lessen esteem for frequent confession realize that what they are doing is alien to the Spirit of Christ and disastrous for the Mystical Body of Our Savior" (encyclical letter, *Mystici Corporis Christi,* N. 88).

Let us renew our devotion for the Blessed Sacrament and that other great sacrament that accompanies us through life, the Holy Sacrament of Confession. When was the last time that you made a good confession? St. Paul constantly insists: "Now is the acceptable time! Now is the day of salvation" (2 Corinthians 6:2)!

"I AM THE BREAD OF LIFE!"

"This is a hard saying; who can believe it?" Jesus was fully aware that his disciples were murmuring in protest at what He had said. When Our Lord promised the Eucharist, as recorded in the sixth chapter of St. John, the vast majority of people would not believe Him. "From then on many of His disciples broke away and walked with Him no more" (John 6:60-61,66).

In His first year of public ministry, Our Divine Savior was an immense success. Thousands flocked to Him as they witnessed astounding wonders. The blind saw; the lame walked; the deaf heard; the dead were raised to life. It was wonderful! St. John notes, however, that many were interested only in the miracles and wonders that He performed. "A vast crowd kept following him because they saw the signs he was performing on the sick" (John 6:2).

Our Lord's Mission Was The Redemption

The Second Person of the Blessed Trinity did not become Man to be a political, a sociological or an economic redeemer. His mission was not to heal bodies. Our Blessed Lord wanted the people's faith, faith in His Messianic mission, faith that He was the promised Messiah. Indeed, He did heal because of the enormity of His merciful compassion. Always, however, His healing was related to faith in His Messianic mission. That is the reason that when "they were going to come and carry him off to make him king, he withdrew again to the mountain alone" (John 6:15). The kingdom of Jesus Christ is not of this world!

Our Lord's mission was the Redemption, atonement to the Father for the sins of the world. He is the promised Messiah Who restores the order that was destroyed by the sin of our first parents (see Genesis 3:15). Jesus Christ is the "ransom" Who saves us from the bondage of sin, the dominion of Satan and the punishment of death, eternal death. Our Blessed Lord is the "Lamb of God Who takes away the sins of the world."

"I am The Bread Of Life!"

Because He demanded faith, Jesus put His followers to the supreme test. "I am the Bread of Life," He said. There was no mistaking the words which He repeated consistently: "I am the Bread of Life . . . I am the living Bread that comes down from heaven; whoever eats this Bread will live forever; the Bread that I give is my Flesh for the life of the world" (John 6:48-51).

The Jews completely understood His words and their tremendous implication. St. John tells us that they began to quarrel: "How can this man give us His flesh to eat?" Yet, Our Lord insisted: "Amen, amen, I say to you, unless you eat the flesh of the Son of Man and drink his blood you do not have life within you. Whoever eats my flesh and drinks my blood has eternal life and I will raise him up on the last day. For my flesh is true food and my blood is true drink. Whoever eats my flesh and drinks my blood remains in me and I in him. Just as the Father who has life sent me and I have life because of the Father so the man who feeds on me will have life because of me. This is the bread that comes down from heaven. Unlike your ancestors who ate and died nonetheless, the man who eats this bread shall live forever" (John 6:53-58).

"Yet, One Of You Is A Devil!"

With the announcement of the Eucharist, Our Lord's success suddenly seemed doomed to failure. "This is a hard saying; who can believe it?" When Jesus announced the Eucharist, He lost the masses for "many turned and walked with Him no more."

One Apostle watched in disbelief and dismay. It was Judas Iscariot. St. John informs us that his heart was already drenched in sin. He was a thief (see John 12:6). When Jesus lost the crowd, Judas Iscariot, in his hardness of heart, lost faith in the Lord. Why? He refused to believe in the Eucharist! Chosen to be an Apostle, he was now "a devil" (see John 6:70-71).

An important lesson must be learned in Judas Iscariot's lack of faith. The Eucharist is the Supreme Gift given us by Our Blessed Lord. He gives us Himself! We must believe Him! We must adore and love His Eucharistic Presence by living a life that is "worthy of the Gospel of Christ" (Philippians 1:27). He commands us to "eat His Body and drink His Blood." Consequently, the Church has always exhorted Christ's faithful to receive Holy Communion frequently. The Eucharist is, as the Second Vatican Council teaches, the "source and the summit" of all the sacraments. "Really partaking of the Body of the Lord in the breaking of the Eucharistic Bread, we are taken into communion with Him and with one another" (*Lumen Gentium,* N. 7).

"Master, To Whom Shall We Go?"

Not all left the Lord when He announced the Eucharist. St. John says that some faithful disciples remained with the Lord. Perhaps they did not understand; perhaps their faith was still weak. Yet, they stayed. They took Jesus at His word. Then, "Jesus said to the Twelve, 'Do you also wish to leave?'" Peter spoke for us that day. "Master, to whom shall we go? You have the words of eternal life" (John 6:69).

The Savior, saddened by those that had left, cherished Peter's reply from the depth of His Heart. Like Peter, we also must believe. The Blessed Sacrament is the Body and Blood of Jesus Christ. It is, as the Second Vatican

Council teaches, "the memorial of (Christ's) death and Resurrection, a sacrament of love, a sign of unity, a bond of charity, a paschal banquet in which Christ is eaten, the mind is filled with grace, and a pledge of future glory is given to us" (*Constitution on the Liturgy,* N. 47).

Because she is the Mother of the Lord, Mary is Our Lady of the Most Blessed Sacrament. May Our Blessed Mother inspire us, her wayward children, to love her Son, Jesus, in the Most Holy Eucharist.

"HOLY COMMUNION IS JESUS!"

Have you seen the recent polls taken among Catholics? The statistics are astounding. Seventy percent of American Catholics do not believe in the Real Presence of Jesus Christ in the Holy Eucharist. One might dispute the polls' accuracy or doubt that the terminology used was properly understood. Yet, when one considers the lack of devotion and respect that is shown to the Eucharist, one readily admits that there is a grave problem.

Disbelief in the Real Presence is nothing new. When St. John described the promise of the Eucharist, he noted that "many of his disciples broke away and walked with him no more" (John 6:66). Two thousand years later, this lack of faith still remains.

Symbolic Or Real

Some time ago, I preached at a Forty-Hours Devotion at a large parish in the East. A few of the teachers asked me to address the seventh and eighth grade pupils of the parish school. I asked the students this question: "Is the presence of Jesus in the Blessed Sacrament real or is it symbolic?" A sheepish look flashed on their faces. I knew there was a problem. Finally, a young man raised his hand. "Symbolic," he said! There was a thud in my heart. I asked if he understood what the word, symbolic, meant. "Yes," he said. "It means that a thing stands for something that it really isn't." An air of agreement filled the room. Sad to say, they simply were not aware of the Real Presence of Jesus Christ in the Holy Eucharist. I spent the next hour explaining the Church's teaching on the Real Presence to them.

Later, their completely dismayed teacher told me that the boy who answered was the brightest student in the school. She insisted that she had followed carefully the catechism approved by their diocese. Yet, her Catholic instincts told her that something was wrong. "The catechism," she said, "hardly ever refers to the Real Presence of Our Lord in the Eucharist, if at all." When will we admit that today's catechetics, with rare exceptions, are a complete catastrophe?

The Real Presence

We must be unambiguously clear! *THE PRESENCE OF OUR LORD JESUS CHRIST IN THE BLESSED SACRAMENT IS REAL! IT IS NOT SYMBOLIC!* The *Catechism of the Catholic Church* leaves no doubt. "In the Most Blessed Sacrament of the Eucharist the 'Body and Blood, together with the Soul and Divinity of our Lord Jesus Christ and therefore the whole Christ is truly, really, and substantially contained'" (N. 1374).

The Catechism also footnotes the teachings of the Council of Trent, 1551 A.D., which is even more emphatic. "If anyone denies that in the Sacrament of the Most Holy Eucharist there are truly, really, and substantially contained the Body and Blood together with the Soul and Divinity of our Lord Jesus Christ, and therefore the whole Christ, but shall say that He is in it as by a sign or figure, or force, let him be anathema."

One simply cannot remain a Catholic and refuse belief in the Real Presence of Jesus in the Blessed Sacrament! As is evident in the sixth chapter of John, Our Divine Lord demands belief in the Eucharist.

"My Flesh Is Real Food!"

Perhaps a personal experience will make theological language more clear. The incident took place on the Papago Indian Reservation, about fifty miles from Tucson, Arizona. Some of the Papago Indians have the custom of instructing their own children in the Faith. One day a woman came to me with her seven-year-old daughter. She assured me that her child was prepared to make her First Confession and receive her First Holy Communion.

"I have one question," I said to the child. "What is Holy Communion?" Without hesitation the little girl answered: "Holy Communion is Jesus." Not even St. Thomas Aquinas, the Angelic Doctor, could have surpassed the precision and wisdom of her simple answer: "Holy Communion is Jesus!"

It was my profound privilege to give this child her First Holy Communion that Sunday. She approached the altar dressed in white with a veil on her head. "The Body of Christ," I said as I placed the Body of Jesus on her tongue. With folded hands and bowed head, she responded "Amen." She took Our Blessed Lord at His word and believed! In that wonderful moment, she possessed the Lord and He possessed her, completely. Jesus and the child were united in an unsurpassable intimacy!

This is precisely the faith that Our Blessed Lord expects from us. We must take our Lord at His word and believe! Faith in the Real Presence of Jesus Christ in the Eucharist is the *sine qua non* condition of Catholic faith. One cannot be Catholic without belief in the Real Presence. Faith in the Eucharist is the dividing line between true followers of Jesus Christ and those who pay Him mere lip service.

When we receive Holy Communion, may our Amen always be a sign of firm faith in the Real Presence. Remember the lesson of the Papago Indian girl: "Holy Communion is Jesus." This childlike faith is most pleasing to Our Blessed Lord. From the depth of His Sacred Heart, Jesus will bestow countless blessings on us. The Heart of Jesus is an infinite fount of mercy and love which He showers upon us in the Holy Eucharist. "O Sacrament Most Holy, O Sacrament Divine! All praise and all thanksgiving be every moment thine!"

"THOU ART THE CHRIST, THE SON OF GOD!"

"How can this man give us his flesh to eat" (John 6:52)? This question was asked by the Jews who refused to believe in the Eucharist. Our Blessed Lord was asking them to take a tremendous leap of faith. Nevertheless, it was one that they should have taken because the signs were evident. When John the Baptist's disciples asked Jesus if He was the promised Messiah, He said: "Go and tell John what you hear and see: the blind regain their sight, the lame walk, lepers are cleansed, the deaf hear, the dead are raised, and the poor have the good news proclaimed to them. Blessed is the one who takes no offense in me" (Matthew 11:4-6).

Jesus Christ Is The Messiah

Jesus had performed all of the messianic signs foretold by the prophets (see Isaiah 26:19; 29:18-19; 35:5-6; 61:1). No one seeking truth could have failed to recognize them. Jesus Christ should have been believed. The High Priest and the members of the Sanhedrin were beyond excuse because of their refusal to acknowledge Him as the Promised Messiah (see John 10:26,16:6).

Indeed, they acted in ignorance as both St. Peter and St. Paul attest (see Acts 3:17 & 1 Corinthians 2:8). But, as the Fathers of the Church comment, their ignorance was due to their own false ideas regarding the Messiah, their extreme hatred of Jesus, and their hardness of heart in rejecting His teachings. The fulfillment of the prophecies, the testimony of His miracles and His whole ministry were irrefutable proofs of the authenticity of His messianic mission. His every action was aimed at the glory of the Father and the salvation of mankind. Clearly, they were responsible for their ignorance. The only exceptions recorded by the Evangelists were Nicodemus, the Pharisee "who came to Jesus at night," (John 3:2) and Joseph of Arimathea, "a good and just man (who) had not consented to (the Sanhedrin's) doings" (Luke 23:50-51).

"My Flesh is real food and My Blood is real drink," Our Lord insisted. Only three possibilities could explain such a curious claim. Jesus Christ was a deceiver, He was mad or He truly had divine power. We know that Our Lord was no ordinary man! Our faith assures us that He is the Messiah, the Son of God.

True God And True Man

The Heavenly Father Himself confirmed Our Lord's divinity at His Baptism. When Jesus emerged from the waters of the Jordan River, the Holy Spirit descended upon Him in the form of a dove. "A voice came from the heavens saying, 'This is my beloved Son, with whom I am well pleased'" (Matthew 3:17).

At Sunday Mass we say: "For us men and for our salvation, He came down from heaven and became Man." We believe that the Second Person of the Blessed Trinity, the Eternal Word of God, assumed a human nature and became Man. The *Catechism of the Catholic Church* teaches: "The unique and altogether singular event of the Incarnation of the Son of God does not mean that Jesus Christ is part God and part man, nor does it imply that he is the result of a confused mixture of the divine and the human. He became truly Man while remaining truly God. Jesus Christ is true God and true Man" (N. 464).

Our Lord was fully conscious of His divinity from the first moment of His conception in the womb of the Blessed Virgin. Thus, standing by the Sea of Galilee, He could assert: "Unless you eat my body and drink my blood, you will not have life in you" (John 6:52). Our Blessed Lord was speaking with the authority and power of the Son of God. Being divine, He could neither deceive nor be deceived. St. Cyril of Alexandria said: "Do not doubt whether this is true, but rather receive the words of the Savior in faith, for, since He is the Truth, He cannot lie."

The Multiplication Of The Loaves

To illustrate Our Lord's divine power, St. John relates two astonishing miracles which occurred immediately before the announcement of the Eucharist. Five thousand men, not including women and children, were gathered to hear Jesus speak. He asked Philip to buy food for the people. "Not even with two hundred days' wages could we buy loaves to give each of them a mouthful," Philip replied. Andrew observed a lad with "five barley loaves and a couple of dried fish." The Master said: "Tell the people to sit down." Not only did He feed everyone, but to the amazement of all, twelve baskets were left over. Only a Person Who has divine power could have accomplished this astounding miracle.

Shortly after this telling event, the Apostles set out to sea without Jesus. Suddenly, in the still of the darkness, "they sighted Jesus approaching the boat, walking on the water." This is another astonishing proof of the divine power of the Lord Jesus. "Do not be afraid, it is I," Jesus said (John 6:19-20). He assures us as well!

If we truly believe in Jesus Christ, we must believe all that the Catholic Church teaches regarding the Eucharist. Whenever doubts arise, recall the words of Peter when the crowd abandoned Jesus. Our Lord asked the Apostles: "Do you want to leave me, too?" Simon Peter spoke for all: "Lord, to whom shall we go? You have the words of eternal life and we have believed and have come to know that thou art the Christ, the Son of the living God" (John 6:69-70). Yes, Lord Jesus! To whom else shall we go?

St. Peter Julian Eymard, the great champion of the Eucharist, challenges our faith. "Let us firmly believe in the Real Presence of Jesus Christ in the Eucharist! Jesus

Christ is there! When we enter a Church, a feeling of respect should come upon us, a respect of faith and love on meeting Jesus Christ in Person; for it is indeed He Whom we are meeting."

Whenever we enter a Catholic church, let us recall that, contained in the tabernacle is He Whom the heavens cannot contain. Silently waiting for us is the King of kings, the Lord of lords, Jesus Christ, the Son of God! Come! Let us adore Him!

"SOUL OF CHRIST, SANCTIFY ME!"

In 1965 Pope Paul VI issued the encyclical letter *Mysterium Fidei,* The Mystery of Faith. It is a wonderful synthesis of the Church's teachings on the Eucharist as Sacrifice and Sacrament. "The Eucharist is an ineffable gift," Pope Paul said, "which the Church received from Christ her Spouse as a pledge of His immense love." He cited the teachings of the Second Vatican Council which exhorted Christ's faithful to offer the Eucharist with the priest "as a sacrifice for their own salvation and that of the world, and to find in it spiritual nourishment."

The Holy Father also proposed various means of fostering Eucharistic worship which will prove extremely beneficial to our reflections. Let us examine a few.

Daily Mass And Communion

"It is greatly desired," Pope Paul said, "that the faithful, every day and in great numbers, participate in the Sacrifice of the Mass (and) receive Holy Communion with a pure heart, giving thanks to Christ Our Lord for so great a gift." He quoted the teachings of his predecessor, Pope Saint Pius X who said: "The desire of Jesus Christ and of the Church that all the faithful receive daily Communion means above all that through the sacramental union with God they may obtain the strength necessary for mastering their passions, for purifying themselves of their daily venial faults and for avoiding the grave sins to which human frailty is exposed."

In every parish there is a handful of people who attend daily Mass. Others attend during Lent and Advent. Undoubtedly, daily Mass is the most effective means for growing in love of the Eucharist. Imagine! Each day one can stand at the foot of the Cross with Our Blessed Mother, John and Mary Magdalene and participate in the Mass, that great memorial of our Redemption.

In Holy Communion, the Bread of Angels literally becomes "our daily Bread." Our Blessed Lord said: "Come to me all you that labor and find life burdensome and I will refresh you. Take my yoke upon your shoulders and learn from me for I am meek and gentle of heart. You will find rest for your souls" (Matthew 11:28-29).

Why not begin the marvelous practice of daily Mass and Communion immediately? Blessings and graces will flow with the generosity that only Our Divine Lord can provide. What better way is there to become Christlike than through the Holy Eucharist?

Daily Visits To The Blessed Sacrament

Pope Paul VI also strongly encouraged daily visits to Our Lord in the Blessed Sacrament. "In the course of the day the faithful should not omit to visit the Blessed Sacrament, which according to the liturgical laws must be kept in the churches with great reverence in a most honorable location. Such visits are a proof of gratitude, an expression of love, and an acknowledgment of the Lord's presence."

An expression of love! Much is said of Our Lord's love for us, individually. He Himself pointed this out often. "There is no greater love than this: to lay down one's life for one's friend." Then Our Lord added those wonderful words, addressed to each of us: "You are my friends" (John 15:12).

Make no mistake, however! Jesus Christ wants us to love Him in return! Recall His question to Peter before He conferred the papacy on him. "Simon, Son of John, do you love me?" (John 21:16) Three times, Our Lord asked him, so much did He want Peter's love. He asks us the same haunting question: "Do you love me?" How can we respond positively if we are too busy to visit Him in the tabernacle?

24

Let us make time for visits to Jesus in the Blessed Sacrament. Countless blessings are sure to follow for the Savior will not be outdone in generosity. We give Him an hour; He returns an eternity. "I love those who love me; those who seek me eagerly shall find me . . . With me are riches and honor, lasting wealth and justice. The fruit I give is better than the finest gold, the return I make is better than pure silver" (Proverbs 8:17-19).

"Close To You Bid Me"

When we visit Our Lord, hidden in the tabernacle, we find peace. This is especially true in times of distress. The peace of Christ enters our souls. "My peace I give you. I do not give it to you as the world gives peace. Do not be distressed or fearful" (John 14:27).

As we see the flickering sanctuary light sway in the silence of the sanctuary, we know that we are alone with Jesus. A spiritual communion takes place as He enters our hearts. His Presence fills us with a sweetness that replaces the sadness of this jaded, weary world.

Our Lord, Who is usually alone, is always pleased to see us. One can pray: "O Divine Jesus, alone and lonely in so many tabernacles throughout the world, I offer You my poor heart and my imperfect love. Make every moment of my life, every beat of my heart, an act of love for You.

"Lord Jesus, You never weary in Your constant quest for sinners. Through the Immaculate Heart of Mary, accept my poor prayers. I offer them to You through her hands, in reparation for my sins and the sins of others. Jesus, my Lord and my God, I love You!"

Jesus is the lonely prisoner of love hidden in the tabernacle. Close to Him in the Most Blessed Sacrament, let us pray the *Anima Christi* of St.Ignatius Loyola:

25

Soul of Christ, sanctify me;
Body of Christ, save me;
Blood of Christ, inebriate me;
Water from the side of Christ, wash me;
Passion of Christ, strengthen me;
O good Jesus, hear me;
Within Your wounds, hide me;
Separated from You, let me never be;
From the evil one, protect me;
At the hour of my death, call me,
And close to You bid me,
That with Your saints,
I may praise You forever and ever.
Amen!

OUR LADY OF THE MOST BLESSED SACRAMENT

What a marvelous title! Our reflections on the Eucharist would be totally inadequate unless we considered the unique role of Our Blessed Mother in the mystery. In every age, the Mother of God reveals her Son's Eucharistic Presence to us. She is near every tabernacle. She kneels with us in adoration before the Holy Eucharist. Truly, Mary is Our Lady of the Most Blessed Sacrament.

Mary Is Linked To The Holy Eucharist

The relationship between Mary and the Eucharist is evident in the Gospels. Bishop Fabian Bruskewitz of the Diocese of Lincoln attested to this wonderfully in his recent article on the Immaculate Conception. "There are many ways in which Mary is linked to the Holy Eucharist. It was, after all, she who gave to God the body and blood that He joined to the soul of Jesus, which He created and then united to His divinity in her womb. This is the Body, Blood, Soul and Divinity of Christ that we receive in Holy Communion" (Southern Nebraska Register, December 9, 1994).

"Behold The Handmaid Of The Lord"

The Archangel Gabriel, "sent from God," salutes Mary, a Jewish maiden of fifteen. One of the highest angels of the heavens was chosen as God's ambassador to bring Mary the glad tidings. Will she give the Messiah a human nature? Will she be the mother who will bear the Promised Redeemer of Man? The Blessed Trinity, Father, Son and Holy Spirit, await her answer. Gabriel and the whole heavenly court await. Mankind awaits. In the inscrutable designs of Almighty God, He will not put His plan of redemption into motion without the consent of the Virgin.

In an act of perfect obedience and humility, Mary, the New Eve, surrenders her will totally to the will of God. Without hesitation she responds: "Behold the handmaid of the Lord. Be it done unto me according to thy word" (Luke 1:38). And the Word was made Flesh! God became Man! His mission of our salvation begins in the Virgin Mary's womb.

Never had God been so completely pleased with one of His children. Never again will He be so pleased. Mary is the apple of the Father's eye (Psalm 17:8). Can it not be said that it was precisely at this moment of the Annunciation that Our Blessed Mother made her First Holy Communion? At the instant of her "Fiat," she became the living tabernacle of the Most High God!

"Thine Own Soul A Sword Shall Pierce"

The spirit of Christmas Season continues with the Feast of the Presentation. The liturgy pronounces the Babe of Bethlehem to be the Light of the World! Conforming to the Law of Moses, Joseph and Mary bring the Child to the Temple and offer Him to God. Led by the Holy Spirit, Simeon recognizes Mary's Son as the Messiah. With trembling hands, he takes Jesus from her arms. As he holds the Lord, he is engulfed in the mystery of the Incarnation. "Now You can dismiss Your servant in peace," he prays. "My eyes have seen Your salvation."

Simeon then turns to Our Blessed Lady and says to her: "This Child is destined to be the downfall and the rise of many in Israel, a sign of contradiction; and your own soul, a sword shall pierce" (Luke 2:34-35). In that moment, St. Alphonsus de Liguori reflects that Mary saw Calvary. She saw that, in God's plan of the Redemption, her Son would have to offer His life on the Cross. Thirty-three years later, Simeon's prophesy came to pass on Calvary. The sword severely pierced her Immaculate Heart as "she stood by the Cross."

Jesus is the Light of the World Who comes to us in Holy Communion. As Mary handed Him to Simeon, she presents Him to us in the Holy Eucharist. When Jesus comes to us in Holy Communion, may we receive Him with some share of the devotion of Mary and Joseph. May we take Him into our arms with the same love and devotion of that "just and pious man," Simeon.

The Worthy Associate Of The Redeemer

In the encyclical *Marialis Cultis,* Pope Paul VI teaches that the liturgical renewal has "properly considered the Blessed Virgin in the mystery of Christ, and, in harmony with tradition, has recognized the singular place that belongs to her in Christian worship as the holy Mother of God and the worthy Associate of the Redeemer" (N.15).

The rich meaning of Pope Paul's words becomes clearer as we reflect on the scene at Calvary. "Now there stood by the cross of Jesus, his mother" (John 19:25). Suffering with her Son, Mary endures an agony beyond all telling. Pope Pius XII explained it in this way: "(On Calvary) Mary bore with courage and confidence the tremendous burdens of her sorrows and desolation. Truly, the Queen of Martyrs, more than all the faithful 'filled up those things that are wanting of the sufferings of Christ for the sake of His Body, which is the Church'" (*Mystici Corporis,* N.110).

Many Catholics hold that Mary, by the will of Jesus Christ, is the Co-Redemptrix of the human race. Her role in His Redemptive act was not necessary but our Lord willed that she unite her sufferings at the foot of the Cross with His. Thus Our Lady, the worthy Associate of the Redeemer, teaches us the true meaning of participation at Mass. As she stood by the Cross of Calvary, she stands by us at every Sacrifice of the Mass. Our Blessed Lady inspires us to bring our own crosses to the Mass. There, we place them in her loving hands. Mary, Our Mother of Sorrows, teaches us to unite our sufferings with her Son's sufferings, "for the sake of his body, which is the Church" (Colossians 1:24).

Our Divine Lord told us: "Whoever wishes to be my disciple must deny his very self, take up his cross each day, and follow in my steps" (Luke 9:24). He sends us crosses but He does not let us carry them alone. He is with us; Mary is with us. When we unite our sufferings with the "sufferings of Christ," then the trials and tribulations of this life take on tremendous significance. This is the reason that the saints welcomed sufferings. By their sufferings, they were united with Christ. At the Holy Sacrifice of the Mass, when the priest lifts the paten and offers Jesus, the Sacred Victim, to the Heavenly Father, let us unite our crosses with His. Then, participation becomes a living reality.

Blessed Mother in heaven, because of our sins, the "sword pierced your heart." In atonement, Jesus suffered and died on the Cross. We come to you with true sentiments of repentance. Teach us to truly participate in the Holy Sacrifice of the Mass. Teach us to love your Divine Son in the Blessed Eucharist!

"MARY! A TEMPLE MORE MAGNIFICENT THAN SOLOMON'S!"

The renowned liturgist Father Pius Parsch wrote of Our Lady: "God prepared a temple for His Son, more beautiful than Solomon's, the body and soul of Mary Immaculate. See what tremendous vistas open before the mind trying to appreciate Mary's grace and dignity." Let us explore those "vistas" and their relation to the Blessed Eucharist.

Each year on February 11 the Church commemorates the Memorial of Our Lady of Lourdes. The opening prayer guides us in preparation for a worthy reception of Holy Communion: "May the prayers of the sinless Mother of God help us to rise above our human weakness." This short oration urges us to imitate Our Blessed Mother in preparation for the worthy reception of the Eucharist.

The Immaculate One

On the Feast of the Annunciation in the year 1858, after sixteen apparitions, "the Lady" identified herself to Bernadette Soubirous. She said: "*I am the Immaculate Conception!*" It was a startling revelation! From the moment of her conception in the womb of her mother, St. Anne, Mary was preserved free from original sin. Never did Mary come under the dominion of Satan, not for an instant. Moreover, throughout her earthly life, Our Blessed Mother never sinned! St. Augustine said that every personal sin must be excluded from her. St. Thomas Aquinas, the Angelic Doctor, was equally clear: "We must confess that the Blessed Virgin never committed an actual sin, neither mortal nor venial . . . 'Thou art all fair, O my love, and there is not a spot in thee'" (Canticle of Canticles 4:7).

Imagine! In all mankind's sad story of sin, Mary is the only sinless one. Consequently, Gabriel greeted her as "full of grace." Mary, the New Eve, practiced every virtue to the highest degree possible. She was perfectly pleasing to the Heavenly Father. Our Blessed Mother is the Virgin most humble, the Virgin most obedient, the Virgin most pure.

St. Theresa of the Child Jesus explained Mary's "fullness of grace" in her own charming way. She said that one could take a glass of any size, and fill it to the brim so that even one additional drop would spill over. The glass would be completely full. That is how perfectly pleasing Our Blessed Lady is to God. She could not possibly be more pleasing, more "full of grace."

With joy we welcome the wonderful words of the poet Wordsworth:

> *"Woman! Above all women glorified;*
> *Our tainted nature's solitary boast;*
> *Purer than foam on central ocean tost."*

Mary Is Our Mother And Our Model

Pope John Paul II, following the teachings of the Second Vatican Council, says that Mary is both Mother and Model of all the faithful. Therefore, she must be our model of Eucharistic devotion because she was found "worthy" to receive the Son of God in her sacred womb.

The Church teaches that Christ's faithful must be free from mortal sin before receiving Holy Communion. However, freedom from mortal sin is only the beginning of Eucharistic preparation. In imitation of Mary, we also must strive to receive Our Lord in Holy Communion as worthily as we possibly can. Like Our Lady, we should attempt to free ourselves from even the slightest venial sin.

Purging Ourselves From Sin

Sacred Scripture records no meeting between the Blessed Virgin and St. Paul. Who would doubt, however, that the Apostle was devoted to Our Blessed Mother? Was she not Mother and Model for Paul as well? Can we not see her motherly influence in the Apostle's magnificent plea to the Colossians? "Put to death whatever in your nature is rooted in earth: fornication, uncleanness, passion, evil desires, and that lust which is idolatry. Because of these sins, the wrath of God is coming upon the disobedient. By these sins you too once conducted yourselves when you lived in that way. But now you must put them all away: anger, fury, malice, slander and obscene language out of your mouths. Stop lying to one another since you have taken off the old man with his practices and have put on the new man who is being renewed, for knowledge, in the image of the Creator" (Colossians 3:5-10).

"You Are God's Chosen Ones, Holy And Beloved"

After having put aside the "old self" of sin, St. Paul then urges putting on the "new man" of virtuous living. "Because you are God's chosen ones, holy and beloved, clothe yourselves with heartfelt mercy, kindness, humility, meekness, and patience. Bear with each other; forgive whatever grievances you have against one another. Forgive as the Lord has forgiven you. Above all these virtues put on love, which binds the rest together and makes them perfect. And let the peace of Christ control your hearts, the peace into which you were called into one body . . . Whatever you do, in word or deed, do everything in the name of the Lord Jesus, giving thanks to God the Father through him" (Colossians 3:12-17).

The Church does not ask us simply to admire the virtues of Our Blessed Mother. She challenges us to imitate her. Mary is the new Eve, the completely new creation made in the image of the Father. On the Solemnity of her glorious Assumption into heaven, the Church prays: "Today the Virgin Mother of God was taken up into heaven. She is the beginning and the pattern of the Church in its perfection" (Preface of the Mass of the Assumption).

Avoiding sin and practicing the virtues is a lifelong battle for us. Yet, true Eucharistic preparation requires that we accept St. Paul's demand to live a life "worthy of the Gospel of Christ" (Philippians 1:27). Our Lady gives us a mother's example.

In his Angelus message of December 8, 1994, the Holy Father teaches this clearly: "Immaculate Mary's fullness of grace also reminds us of the immense possibilities for goodness, beauty, greatness and joy which are within reach of human beings when they let themselves be guided by God's will and reject sin."

Despite our human weakness and constant failures, let us turn to Mary, Our Beloved Queen, Our Advocate, the Mediatrix of all graces and dispenser of all God's treasures. Blessed Mother in heaven, teach us, your children, to know and love our Eucharistic Lord. Teach us to receive Jesus in the Most Blessed Sacrament as worthily as we possibly can! O MARY, CONCEIVED WITHOUT SIN, PRAY FOR US WHO HAVE RECOURSE TO THEE!

THE HOLY EUCHARIST IS "A SIGN OF UNITY"
Part One - The Papal Magisterium

The Second Vatican Council teaches that the Holy Eucharist is "a sacrament of love, a sign of unity, a bond of charity, and a paschal banquet in which Christ is eaten" (*Document on Liturgy,* N. 47). On February 22 the Church commemorates the Feast of the Chair of St. Peter. In this liturgy, the Church reminds Catholics of the necessity of obedience to the Papal Magisterium. Therefore, let us consider fidelity to the teaching office of the Pope and its link to the Eucharist as "a sign of unity."

The Second Person of the Blessed Trinity became Man in Jesus Christ. Our Blessed Savior is True God and True Man. His mission was the Redemption, atonement to the Father for the sins of the world. He accomplished this on the Cross of Calvary. Our Blessed Lord willed that His saving work should be carried on until the end of time by a visible body. That visible body, founded by Our Lord, is the Roman Catholic Church. Jesus Christ is the "Chief Shepherd" of this body of believers (see 1 Peter 5:4).

"Upon This Rock!"

The Gospel for the Mass of the Chair of St. Peter records Jesus Christ's promise to Peter: "Thou art Peter and upon this rock I will build my Church and the gates of hell shall not prevail against you. I will entrust to you the keys of the Kingdom of Heaven. Whatever you bind on earth shall be bound in heaven and whatever you loose on earth shall be loosed in heaven" (Matthew 16:18-19). Reflecting on Our Blessed Lord's words, Pope John Paul teaches that: "The opposing terms 'binding-loosing' serve to show the totality of the power" (General Audience Nov. 25, 1992).

The Feast of the Chair of St. Peter is a liturgical reminder of this undeniable reality. Jesus Christ is "the

Head of his body, which is the Church" (Ephesians 5:23). Our Lord, however, has ascended into heaven; He is no longer with us in His physical presence. So, He left someone here in His place, someone that we could see and hear. Jesus Christ chose Simon Peter to stand in His place. He made Peter the visible head of His Church.

The Pope is the Vicar of Jesus Christ on earth. A vicar is one who stands in the place of another and acts with his full authority. Therefore, the Holy Father has jurisdiction over the whole Church in its beliefs, moral teachings and discipline. He "is the perpetual and visible source and foundation of the unity both of the bishops and the whole company of the faithful" (*Catechism of the Catholic Church*, N. 882).

Peter Lives In His Successor

The authority of Peter did not end with his death. It is passed on to his successors in the Chair of Peter until Jesus comes again. Peter lives in his successors, Linus, Sixtus, Gregory, Leo, Benedict, Pius, John and Paul. Today, he lives in John Paul II, the Successor of Peter, the Bishop of Rome, the Supreme Pontiff and Christ's Vicar on earth.

Can a person dissent from the Church's Magisterium (Teaching Authority) and still claim to be a Catholic in good standing? Quite simply, NO! Despite the clamor of today's dissidents, the Second Vatican Council is quite clear. Christ's faithful must be united with the Pope in his faith and moral teachings. Catholics must render a full submission of mind and will to the Papal Magisterium, both in his extraordinary Magisterium (i.e., *ex cathedra* teachings) and in his ordinary Magisterium, his day-to-day teachings (see Vatican II, *Document on the Church*, N. 25).

With St. Peter As Our Shepherd

The Oration of the Mass of the Chair of St. Peter

prays: "Lord, accept the prayers and gifts of your Church. With St. Peter as our shepherd, keep us true to the faith he taught and bring us to your eternal kingdom." Despite the Church's prayer, the Holy Father's teaching authority is under violent attack. Many modern Catholics erroneously equate his teachings with mere opinion. They claim that they are free to follow dissenting theologians. Others insist that individual conscience is supreme even when it conflicts with the teachings of the Church. A sister, addressing a parish group of over 200 Catholics, defined conscience as "simply *me* coming to a decision." Let me assure you that this is a total perversion of the teachings of the Second Vatican Council concerning conscience.

This was confirmed by Pope John Paul II when he addressed these unfortunate errors during his pastoral visit to the United States in 1987. He told the American bishops in Los Angeles: "It is sometimes reported that a large number of Catholics today do not adhere to the Church's teachings on many questions, notably sexual and conjugal morality, divorce and remarriage . . . It is sometimes claimed that dissent from the Magisterium is totally compatible with being a "good Catholic" and poses no obstacle to the reception of the sacraments. This is a grave error that challenges the teaching office of the bishops of the United States and elsewhere."

A Sign Of Unity

St. Paul teaches us that "there is one Lord, one faith, one baptism, one God and Father of all" (Ephesians 4:5). Jesus Christ, truly present in the Holy Eucharist, is the source of the Church's unity in faith. The Blessed Sacrament is, so to speak, the divine adhesive that unifies Christ's faithful in the truth of Catholic faith. Dissenting from any part of Catholic belief and moral teaching, as the Holy Father made clear, is a grave sin against faith. It is incompatible, he said, with the worthy reception of Holy Communion.

Under the protection of Mary Immaculate, may we always maintain the "obedience of faith" mandated by our holy Faith (Romans 1:5). Without this obedience to the Papal Magisterium, we can never truly be united with the Eucharistic Lord. God grant that we never fail the test in these days of dissent.

THE HOLY EUCHARIST IS "A SIGN OF UNITY"
Part Two - The Magisterium of the Bishops

St. Paul teaches us that true disciples of the Lord Jesus must have the "obedience of faith" to the Church's teachings (see Romans 1:5; the *Catechism of the Catholic Church,* N.143). We have reflected upon the necessity of obedience to the teachings of the Holy Father so as to participate worthily in the Eucharist. Meditating further upon the Eucharist as "a sign of unity," let us now consider the necessity of obedience to the bishops, the Successors of the Apostles.

The role of proclaiming and defending the Sacred Deposit of Catholic Faith has been entrusted directly to the College of Bishops by Jesus Christ, the Son of God (see Matthew 18:18,28:18). Therefore, the worthy reception of the Eucharist requires obedience to the bishops as they proclaim the Deposit of Faith and lawfully administer their dioceses.

The Magisterium Of The Bishops

The Second Vatican Council teaches that: "The bishops, having been appointed by the Holy Spirit, are successors of the Apostles as pastors of souls. Together with the Supreme Pontiff and under his authority they are sent to continue throughout the ages the work of Christ, the Eternal Pastor" (*Decree on the Office of Bishops,* N.2).

This Magisterium (Teaching Office) of bishops is part of the Deposit of Catholic Faith. In continuity with Sacred Tradition and Scripture, Vatican II teaches that there is unity between the Pope and the College of Bishops. "Just as in accord with the Lord's decree, St. Peter and the rest of the Apostles form *a unique Apostolic College,* so in like fashion the Roman Pontiff, Peter's Successor, and the Bishops, the Successors of the Apostles, are united to one another" (*Constitution on the Church,* N.22).

The Holy Father has supreme and universal power over the entire Church. Our Lord gave to Peter alone the Keys of the Kingdom of Heaven. Thus, the bishops must maintain a hierarchical unity with the Roman Pontiff. "The individual bishops, placed in charge of particular churches, exercise their pastoral government over the portion of the People of God committed to their care, and not over other churches nor the universal Church. But each of them, as a member of the episcopal college and legitimate successor of the Apostles, is obliged by Christ's institution and command to be solicitous for the whole Church. This solicitude, although it is not exercised by an act of jurisdiction, contributes greatly to the advantage of the whole Church. For it is the duty of all bishops to promote and safeguard the unity of faith and the discipline common to the whole Church, to instruct the faithful to love the whole Mystical Body of Christ, especially for its poor and sorrowing members and those who are suffering persecution for justice's sake" (Vatican II, *Constitution on the Church,* N.23).

"By Divine Institution"

The Second Vatican Council teaches that: "Bishops by divine institution have succeeded to the place of the Apostles as shepherds of the Church. He who hears them hears Christ, and he who rejects them, rejects Christ and Him who sent Christ (see Luke 10:16). In the bishops, therefore, for whom priests are assistants, Our Lord Jesus, the Supreme High Priest, is present in the midst of all who believe" (*Constitution on the Church,* N.20 & 21).

Moreover, "Individual bishops who have been entrusted with the care of a particular church - - under the authority of the Supreme Pontiff - - feed their sheep in the name of the Lord as their own, ordinary and immediate pastors, performing for them the office of teaching, sanctifying, and governing" (*Decree on the Office of Bishops,* N.11).

"With Peter And Under Peter"

The Papal Magisterium is Our Lord's gift to the Church. It is a divine guarantee that the Church will never fall into doctrinal error. Vatican II, more firmly than previous councils, recognizes and affirms the supremacy of the Pope's teaching authority. "The college or body of bishops has no authority unless it is understood together with the Roman Pontiff, the Successor of Peter as its head. The Pope's power of primacy over all, both pastors and faithful, remains whole and intact. In virtue of his office, that is the Vicar of Christ and pastor of the whole Church, the Roman Pontiff has full, supreme and universal power over the whole Church. And he is always free to exercise this power. The order of bishops, which succeeds to the College of Apostles and gives this body continued existence, is also the subject of supreme and full power over the universal Church, provided we understand this body together with its head, the Roman Pontiff, and never apart from this head" (*Constitution on the Church,* N. 22).

Bishops, therefore, must teach in unity with the Holy Father. Individually, or as a body, their teachings can never contradict or conflict with the teachings of the Successor of Peter. Bishops must always teach, *"with Peter and under Peter"* (*Decree on the Mission Activity of the Church,* N.38).

St. Thomas Becket, the heroic bishop who died a martyr's death for the Faith, said of this unity with Peter: "It is Peter, surely, to whom major judgments concerning God's people are entrusted, when they are submitted to the Bishop of Rome. Under him, the other officers of mother Church are organized, insofar as they are called to share in his responsibility and exercise the power entrusted to them . . . Who can doubt that the Church of Rome is the head of all churches, the source of Catholic teaching? Who does not know that the keys of the kingdom of heaven were given to Peter? Is not the whole structure of the Church built upon Peter's faith and teaching?" (Office of Readings, December 29)

As we reflect on the Eucharistic mystery, let us affirm our loyalty to the teachings of the Holy Father and the bishops who teach *"with Peter and under Peter."* May Mary, the Holy Mother of God and the Virgin most obedient, teach us to have the humility and the "obedience of faith" required to grow in our devotion to her Divine Son. Truly, the Blessed Eucharist is the "sign of unity," present among us.

THE HOLY SACRIFICE OF THE MASS

A young priest was taking some people on a tour of his church. There was a plaque on the wall of the entrance which stated: "The Holy Sacrifice of the Mass was first offered at Saints Peter and Paul Church on June 29, 1956." The priest then made this curious comment: "This plaque was put here before Vatican II. In the light of the Council, we no longer view the Mass as a sacrifice. It is a meal that commemorates the love of Jesus." There was a feigned nod of approval given by some. Most did not understand the dreadful implications of his remark. Obviously, the priest had never read the documents of the Second Vatican Council.

The Eucharistic Sacrifice

The *Catechism of the Catholic Church,* quoting the Second Vatican Council's Constitution on the Liturgy, clearly defines the Mass in its essence. "At the Last Supper, the night He was betrayed, our Savior instituted the Eucharistic Sacrifice of His Body and Blood. This He did in order to perpetuate the Sacrifice of the Cross throughout the ages until He should come again, and so to entrust to His beloved Spouse, the Church, a memorial of His death and resurrection: A sacrament of love, a sign of unity, a bond of charity, a Paschal banquet 'in which Christ is consumed, the mind is filled with grace, and a pledge of future glory is given to us'" (N.1323).

Removing any doubt concerning the sacrificial nature of the Mass, the *Catechism of the Catholic Church* cites the Council of Trent: "The Sacrifice of Christ and the Sacrifice of the Eucharist are one single sacrifice: 'The Victim is one and the same: the same now offers through the ministry of priests, who then offered Himself on the Cross; only the manner of offering is different.' 'In this divine sacrifice which is celebrated in the Mass, the same Christ who offered Himself once in a bloody manner on the altar of the Cross is now contained and is offered in an unbloody manner'" (N.1367).

The Mediator Between God And Man

Pope Pius XII, already combating the clouds of heresy that were gathering during his pontificate, taught in his encyclical *Mediator Dei*: "The sublime sacrifice of the altar is no mere empty commemoration of the passion and death of Jesus Christ. Rather, it is a true and proper act of sacrifice, whereby the High Priest (Jesus Christ) by an unbloody immolation offers Himself, a most acceptable Victim to the Eternal Father, as He did upon the Cross. It is one and the same Victim; the same Person now offers it by the ministry of His Priests, Who then offered Himself on the Cross, the manner of offering alone being different" (N.68).

The Holy Sacrifice of the Mass is at the heart of Catholicism. St. Thomas Aquinas says: "The whole mystery of our salvation is comprised in the Eucharistic Sacrifice" (*Summa III,* Q83, 2A4). The devil is furious in his attempt to obscure the sacrificial character of the Mass. Why? St. John, the beloved disciple, gives the answer: "The reason the Son of God appeared was to destroy the works of the devil" (1 John 3:8).

Because of Adam's sin, mankind came under the dominion of Satan, the slavery to sin and the punishment of death, eternal death. Jesus Christ is, as Pope Pius XII taught in *Mediator Dei,* the Mediator between God and man. His mission was to restore "the right relationship between man and his Creator." Our Divine Savior restored this order by His Passion and Death on the Cross. "We have a Mediator with the Father, Jesus Christ, the Just One," says St. John. "He is the offering for our sins, not only our sins, but also for the sins of the whole world" (1 John 2:1-2).

Satan, therefore, hates the Cross. He hates the Mass. In his diabolical fury, the evil one never ceases to do all he can to confuse and distort the sacrificial character of the Mass in the minds of Christ's faithful. St. Peter warns us: "Be sober and on your guard because your adversary the devil roams the earth like a roaring lion, seeking whom he may devour. Resist him, strong in the faith" (1 Peter 5:8-9).

A Visible Sacrifice

"The Eucharist is thus a sacrifice because it re-presents (makes present) the Sacrifice of the Cross, because it is its memorial and because it applies its fruits." Quoting the Council of Trent, the Catechism teaches: "(Christ), Our Lord and God, was once and for all to offer Himself to God the Father by His death on the altar of the Cross, to accomplish there an everlasting redemption. But because His priesthood was not to end with His death, at the Last Supper 'on the night when He was betrayed,' (Jesus) wanted to leave to His beloved Spouse, the Church, a visible sacrifice (as the nature of man demands) by which the bloody sacrifice which He was to accomplish once for all on the Cross would be re-presented, its memory perpetuated until the end of the world, and its salutary power be applied to the forgiveness of the sins we daily commit" (N. 1366).

Our Blessed Lord, Jesus Christ, is the Great High Priest and the Victim Who offered Himself up to the Father in atonement for the sins of the world. Jesus is both Priest and Victim at every Mass.

The Eucharist Is Both Sacrifice And Sacrament

The Catholic Church has always taught that the Holy Eucharist is both Sacrifice and Sacrament. At the Holy Sacrifice of the Mass, the Church, from ancient times, always has encouraged the faithful who are properly disposed to partake of the Sacrament. The Blessed Sacrament, in the words of St. Augustine, is the *Paschal Banquet.*

However, the Mass cannot be reduced to a "Communion Service" or a meal separated from the Sacrifice. This was one of the grave heresies of the Protestant Reformers. Martin Luther obstinately rejected the Mass as sacrifice; he insisted that it was only a "Supper" (abendmahl). Because of this, and other heresies, Pope Leo X excommunicated him from the Roman Catholic Church on June 15, 1520.

As we reflect on the Eucharistic Mystery, let us cultivate a deep devotion to the Holy Sacrifice of the Mass. The Mass makes present the Sacrifice of Calvary on our altars. Had it not been for this redemptive act of Our Lord, each one of us would have been hopelessly lost to the slavery of sin, the dominion of Satan and the punishment of death, eternal death. Praised be Jesus Christ, the Great High Priest! He is Our Lord and Savior! He is our Divine Redeemer!

"WE HAVE A GREAT HIGH PRIEST!"

Our Divine Savior, Jesus Christ, is the Great High Priest to Whom St. Paul constantly refers in the Epistle to the Hebrews. "For every high priest taken among men, is ordained for men in the things that appertain to God, that he may offer up gifts and sacrifices for sin" (Hebrews 5:1).

Jesus Christ, the Eternal Word of God Who became Man, is both the Priest and the Victim Who offered Himself up on the Cross of Calvary in atonement for the sins of the world. "It was fitting that we have such a high priest, holy, innocent, undefiled, separated from sinners and made higher than the heavens. He has no need, as did the other high priests, to offer daily sacrifice for their own sins and the sins of others. (Jesus Christ) did that once and for all when he offered himself" (Hebrews 7:26-27).

At every Holy Sacrifice of the Mass this, "once and for all" sacrifice is "re-presented (made present)" on our altars. This dogma is at the heart of Catholic faith. The *Catechism of the Catholic Church* teaches that the Sacrifice of Christ and the Holy Sacrifice of the Mass are *one single sacrifice*. Quoting the Council of Trent (1562 A.D.), it states: "The Victim is one and the same: the same now offers through the ministry of priests, who then offered Himself on the Cross; only the manner of offering is different . . . In this divine sacrifice which is celebrated in the Mass, the same Christ who offered Himself once in a bloody manner on the altar of the Cross is contained and is offered in an unbloody manner" (N. 1367).

Martin Luther, the apostate priest, insisted that the Mass was *not* a sacrifice. He was unyielding in asserting that the Mass is merely a meal where the faithful receive Holy Communion. He further maintained that, at the consecration of the Mass, NO TRANSUBSTANTIATION takes place. Thus, not only did Martin Luther deny the

Mass as Sacrifice, he also denied the Real Presence of Our Lord in the Holy Eucharist as taught by the Catholic Church. This was a terrible perversion of the Faith. The Catholic Church, under the guide of the Holy Spirit, responded quickly and precisely at the Council of Trent.

The Catechism, which, as Pope John Paul II says, is "a statement of the Church's faith and of Catholic doctrine," also responds to the modern heretics. Many theologians and priests have misled Christ's faithful into believing that Vatican II changed the essential character of the Mass. Imitating Luther, they claim that the Mass is only a "meal." I heard one young priest preach that the Mass is no longer a sacrifice because Vatican II so decreed. The Council's document on the liturgy, *Sacrosanctum Concilium,* is clear proof that such statements are utterly irrational, having no basis in truth.

We read in the Catechism: "The Eucharist (Mass) is thus a sacrifice because it *re-presents* (makes present) the Sacrifice of the Cross, because it is its *memorial* and because it *applies* its fruit." Quoting the Council of Trent, the Catechism states: "(Christ), our Lord and God, was once and for all to offer Himself to God the Father by His death on the altar of the Cross, to accomplish there an everlasting redemption. But His priesthood was not to end with His death. At the Last Supper 'on the night He was betrayed,' (He wanted) to leave to His beloved spouse the Church a visible sacrifice (as the nature of man demands) by which the bloody sacrifice which He accomplished once and for all on the Cross would be re-presented, its memory perpetuated until the end of the world, and its salutary power be applied to the forgiveness of sins we daily commit" (N. 1366).

What could be more clear? The Mass is indeed a true and proper sacrifice. Jesus Christ is both the Principal Priest and Victim at every Mass. The priest offers the

Sacrifice of the Mass acting *in persona Christi*, in the very Person of Jesus Christ! After His Ascension, the Great High Priest "has taken his seat at the right hand of the throne of Majesty in heaven" (Hebrews 8:1).

For all eternity, Our Blessed Lord is True God and True Man. Until the end of time, Jesus has left us a living memorial of His Passion and Death on the Cross of Calvary, the Holy Sacrifice of the Mass! It will be offered from the East to the West, from the rising of the sun to its setting until the Lord Jesus comes again in glory. Praised be Jesus Christ, the Redeemer of Man!

"THE EUCHARIST IS ABOVE ALL ELSE A SACRIFICE!"

Every Holy Thursday, Pope John Paul II issues a letter to the priests of the world. His letter of 1980, *Dominicae Cenae,* is exceptionally inspiring. It is a sincere talk "On the Mystery and Worship of the Eucharist." Eloquently, the Holy Father teaches us about the Mystery of the Eucharist as Sacrifice and Sacrament.

The Eucharist Is Sacrifice And Sacrament

Often, there is a tendency to view the Eucharist exclusively as sacrament. The Second Vatican Council, however, reminded Christ's faithful that the Eucharist is both sacrifice and sacrament. The Navarre Commentary on the Code of Canon Law, in fidelity to the Council's teachings, explains that the new Code of Canon Law "wishes to reflect more clearly that the Eucharist is, at the same time, *sacrifice* and *sacrament*." It notes, moreover, that Canon Law "clearly reveals the triple dimension of the Holy Eucharist as 'sacramental sacrifice, sacramental communion and sacramental presence'" (p. 578).

These truths are key, fundamental beliefs of Catholic faith. Yet, despite the inherent beauty of these teachings, many abuses abound in our times. Many Catholics have been saddened by the gratuitous liberties that take place during the Holy Sacrifice of the Mass. The "sense of Catholic faith" has been deeply disturbed. Many dreadful adventures have been imposed on parish liturgies. The range of these abuses has caused much confusion to the Catholic faithful. It is very sad.

The Mass Is The Sacrifice Of Our Redemption

The Holy Sacrifice of the Mass is not a form of entertainment whose purpose is to inflate the egos of vari-

50

ous ministers and the congregation. The Mass is not a vehicle by which we feed our "self-esteem" and come to "feel good about ourselves" in a secular, pop-psychology sense. It certainly is not a social gathering. Neither is it, in its essence and its nature, a meal. Thus, the Holy Sacrifice cannot be viewed only as a communion service, as Martin Luther and his modern followers would insist (See Council of Trent, Session 22, Canon 1).

Alfons Cardinal Stickler, former Cardinal Librarian and Archivist of the Holy See, emphasized this central Eucharistic doctrine in an address given to a seminar sponsored by Christifideles in Newark, New Jersey, May 20, 1995. Commenting on the nature of the Eucharistic Sacrifice, as taught by the Council of Trent (Session 22), His Eminence was clear: "By means of the Consecration (of the Mass) the bread is changed into the Body of Christ and the wine into His Blood. The central intention of (Christ's) Sacrifice is the adoration of God. The Council of Trent specifies that this Sacrifice is not a new one independent from the unique Sacrifice of the Cross. Rather, it is dependent upon the unique Sacrifice of Christ, re-presenting it in a bloodless way such that the Body and Blood of Christ are essential and remain under the appearance of bread and wine."

"Consequently, there is no new sacrificial merit. Rather, it (the merit of the Mass) is infinite through the bloody Sacrifice of the Cross, having been effected, and is realized by Jesus Christ constantly in the Mass. It follows that the action of the Sacrifice consists in the Consecration. The Offertory, by which bread and wine were prepared for the Consecration, and the Communion, the reception of the consecrated Bread or the Body of Christ, are only integral parts of the Mass but they are not essential ones. (The essential part) is the Consecration, by which the priest, in the Person of Christ and in the same way, pronounces the consecrating words of Christ."

"Thus, the Mass is not and cannot simply be a 'Celebration of Communion' or a mere remembrance or memorial of the Sacrifice of the Cross but rather a true unbloody re-presentation of this self-same Sacrifice of the Cross."

Indeed, Our Blessed Lord, through His Church, solemnly invites the faithful to partake of the "Paschal Banquet" at Mass. Yet, as the Pope teaches us in *Dominicae Cenae*: "The Eucharist is above all else a sacrifice. It is the Sacrifice of the Redemption and also the Sacrifice of the New Covenant, as we believe and as the Eastern Churches clearly profess. The Greek Church stated centuries ago: 'Today's sacrifice is like that offered once by the only-begotten Incarnate Word; it is offered by Him now as then since it is one and the same sacrifice'" (N. 9).

In our reflections on the Eucharist, it cannot be stressed strongly enough that the Holy Sacrifice of the Mass *is one with and identical to the Sacrifice of Jesus Christ on the Cross of Calvary!*

"The sacredness of the Mass is not a 'sacralization,' that is to say, something that man adds to Christ's action in the Upper Room, for the Holy Thursday supper was a sacred rite, a primary and constitutive liturgy, through which Christ, by pledging to give His life for us, Himself celebrated sacramentally the mystery of His passion and resurrection, the heart of every Mass" (N. 8).

On the first Holy Thursday night, Our Blessed Savior offered, sacramentally, the identical sacrifice that He would offer on the Cross. In anticipation of Calvary, He offered the first Mass in an unbloody manner. The next day, hanging on the Cross, Jesus, the Great High Priest, offered the Sacrifice of Himself in a bloody manner. In atonement to the Heavenly Father, Our Divine Savior shed the last drop of His Precious Blood for your sins and mine, and the sins of every human being who ever walked the face of the earth.

The Great Amen

Much has been written about the significance of the Great Amen at Holy Mass. In reality the "Amen" expresses our "Yes" to the Eucharist. It affirms our faith in Our Lord's redemptive act on the Cross. Our "Amen" is also an act of faith in His Real Presence in the Blessed Sacrament (see *Inaestimabile Donum*, N. a4).

The Great Amen must also voice our "religious submission of mind and will" to the whole body of Catholic faith and moral teachings. One cannot honestly, before God, exclaim "Amen" at Mass while rejecting the Church's teachings on matters such as the ordination of men only to the priesthood, the transmission of human life as taught in the encyclicals *Humanae Vitae* and *Evangelium Vitae*, the intrinsic evil of homosexual acts, and, indeed, all of Catholic faith and moral teachings. Persons in the state of moral sin should assist at Mass and may benefit from its actual graces, but union with Christ in the Holy Sacrifice of the Mass requires faithful acceptance and adherence to the life and teachings of Christ.

Our "Amen" attests to our obedient solidarity with Jesus Christ and His Holy, Catholic Church. "I beg you," St. Paul urges, "as a prisoner for the Lord, to lead a life worthy of the calling you have received, with perfect humility, meekness, and patience, bearing with one another lovingly. Make every effort to preserve the unity which has the Spirit as its origin and peace as its binding force. There is one body and one Spirit, just as there is one hope given all of you by your call. There is one Lord, one faith, one baptism, one God and Father of all, who is above all and through all and in all" (Ephesians 4:1-6).

In Union With The Saints

At the Holy Sacrifice of the Mass, we offer up our prayers "in union with the whole Church." We become one with the entire Mystical Body of Christ, the *Church Militant* (we here on earth), the *Church Suffering* (the poor souls still being purified in purgatory), and the *Church Triumphant* (Our Blessed Mother and all the saints in heaven).

In 1962, Pope John XXIII placed the name of St. Joseph in the Canon of the Mass. The great St. Joseph is the foster father of Our Lord, the chaste husband of the Virgin Mary and the Church's Universal Patron. May Our Blessed Protector in heaven guide us to a richer understanding and a more profound appreciation of this great re-presentation of our Redemption, the Holy Sacrifice of the Mass.

TRANSUBSTANTIATION

While I was greeting the people after Mass one Sunday morning, a woman approached me with a deep concern. She said that her new pastor had announced that he was moving the tabernacle from the main body of the church. This, he explained, was mandated by the Second Vatican Council. He also made the astounding assertion that Christ's Presence in the Eucharist does not remain after Mass. Based on this assumption, one must conclude that Our Blessed Lord is not present in the consecrated hosts reserved in the tabernacle. Almost in tears, the woman asked if these claims were true.

The Mystery Of Faith

Pope Paul VI addressed these types of pernicious fallacies in his encyclical letter *Mysterium Fidei*. Essentially, the Holy Father restated the teachings of the Council of Trent in the year 1551. The Real Presence of Christ in the Sacred Species *does not cease* after Mass. Any contrary claim is absolutely heretical. Moreover, the Second Vatican Council issued no mandate to move tabernacles.

In *Mysterium Fidei*, Paul VI taught that the Eucharist is reserved in our tabernacles throughout the Universal Church because "beneath the appearance of the species, Christ is contained, the invisible Head of the Church, the Redeemer of the world, the center of all hearts, 'by Whom all things are and by Whom we exist.'"

This is the reason that we genuflect and maintain a respectful silence upon entering a Catholic church. Jesus, the Son of God, is truly present in our tabernacles "beneath the appearance of the species." The Blessed Sacrament, Pope Paul teaches, must be worshiped and adored (see also Council of Trent Session 13, Canons 4 & 6).

Transubstantiation

Pope Paul VI restated the Church's teachings on the doctrine of transubstantiation. Sixteenth century heretics, such as Martin Luther, denied that a substantial change occurred at the Consecration of the Mass. Luther rejected the Church's doctrine of transubstantiation and held that Christ is present simultaneously with the bread.

Ulrich Zwingli held that a "transignification" took place. He said that the bread merely *signifies* the presence of Christ. In fidelity to our Divine Lord's teachings, the Church responded to these heresies quickly and dogmatically.

The Council of Trent infallibly declared that, "by the Consecration of the bread and wine a change is brought about of the whole substance of the bread into the substance of the Body of Christ and the whole substance of the wine into the substance of His Blood. This change the holy Catholic Church properly and appropriately calls transubstantiation" (Session 13, Chapter 4).

At the Consecration of the Mass, the Priest says: "THIS IS MY BODY." In that instant, the bread ceases to be bread. It looks, tastes, smells and feels like bread but it is no longer bread. Bread is substantially changed into the adorable Body of Jesus Christ.

Then the Priest says: "THIS IS THE CUP OF MY BLOOD." Instantly, the wine ceases to be wine. It looks, tastes and smells like wine but it is no longer wine. The wine is substantially changed into the Precious Blood of Our Lord and Savior, Jesus Christ.

Hilaire Belloc, the renowned author and historian, captures Catholic belief in clear, concise language. Catholic doctrine, he writes, is satisfied if one holds that the "whole Humanity and Divinity of Our Lord is present in the Blessed Sacrament after the words of Consecration, and in either element. The original bread and wine wholly cease to be" (See Characters of the Reformation (TAN Books), page 11).

The Doctrine Of Concomitance

Concomitance simply means that the whole Christ, Body, Blood, Soul and Divinity is present under each separate species. When one receives the Sacred Host, one receives the whole Christ, Body, Blood, Soul and Divinity. The same is true of the Precious Blood. When one drinks from the cup, one receives the whole Christ.

St. Robert Bellarmine, a Doctor of the Church, explains the doctrine succinctly: "The Body and Blood of the Lord is consecrated under the two species of bread and wine. Thus, the species of bread represents the Body separated from the Blood, and thus dead. The species of wine represents the Blood separated from the Body. Under both species, however, Christ is present whole and living. The Lord willed that these mysteries preserve in us the constant and daily memory of His venerable passion by which we have escaped every evil and attained every good" (*The Art of Dying Well*, Book Two).

In our times, receiving under both species is often permitted. Great caution must be exercised when distributing from the chalice because of the danger of spilling the Precious Blood. This is especially important when a large number of people receive. Ordinarily, the faithful receive the Sacred Host only. In so doing, they have the absolute assurance that they are receiving the Body, Blood, Soul and Divinity of the Lord Jesus.

Notice the great care taken by priests in purifying the sacred vessels after Communion. The reason is that the Real Presence of Our Lord Jesus remains in each and every visible particle, no matter how small. In the *Lauda Sion*, composed by St. Thomas Aquinas for the Solemnity of *Corpus Christi*, we read: "If the sacrament is broken, have no doubt. Remember there is as much in a fragment as in an unbroken host."

"He Is In Our Midst!"

A review of these fundamental Eucharistic beliefs is needed for the continuing vitality of our faith. Remember that doctrine and devotion are inseparable. Doctrine without devotion is sterile and feeds pride. Devotion not rooted in doctrine, however, leads to excesses and sometimes fanaticism. St. Augustine put forth the formula of "faith seeking understanding." This is one of the purposes of these reflections. Our faith is "seeking understanding."

In the encyclical *Mysterium Fidei*, Paul VI inspires us to love the Blessed Eucharist by blending doctrine and devotion. "No one can fail to understand," he writes, "that the Divine Eucharist bestows upon the Christian people an incomparable dignity. Not only while the sacrifice is being offered and the sacrament received, but as long as the Eucharist is kept in our churches and oratories, Christ is truly Emmanuel, that is 'God with us.' Day and night He is in our midst; He dwells with us, full of grace and truth. He restores morality, nourishes virtues, consoles the afflicted, and strengthens the weak. He gives His own example to those who come to Him that they may all learn to be, like Himself, meek and humble of heart and to seek not their own interests but those of God."

May the Heart of Jesus, in the Most Blessed Sacrament, be praised, adored and loved, with grateful affection, at every moment, in all the tabernacles of the world, even to the end of time. Amen!

"YOU ARE A ROYAL PRIESTHOOD!"

The Second Vatican Council instructed Christ's faithful not to attend the Holy Sacrifice of the Mass merely "as strangers or silent spectators." There must be a *"devout and active participation of the faithful"* (*Constitution on the Liturgy*, N. 50). "(The people) should be instructed by God's word and nourished at the table of the Lord's Body, giving thanks to God. By offering the Immaculate Victim (Jesus Christ) not only through the hands of the priest, but also with him, they should learn to offer themselves. Through Christ, the Mediator, they should be drawn day by day into ever more perfect union with God and with each other, so that God may be all in all" (*Constitution on the Liturgy*, N. 48).

We read in the *Catechism of the Catholic Church*: "The Sunday Eucharist is the foundation and confirmation of all Christian practice. For this reason the faithful are obliged to participate in the Eucharist on days of obligation, unless excused for a serious reason (for example, illness, the care of infants) or dispensed by their own pastor. Those who deliberately fail in this obligation commit a grave sin" (N. 2181).

Participation at the Holy Sacrifice is nothing new, having its origins from apostolic times (see 1 Peter 2:9). In recent times, however, some Catholics have identified liturgical participation *solely* with performing certain functions such as cantors, readers, extraordinary ministers and acolytes. Others unjustly accuse the Church of being discriminatory because the priesthood is open only to men. These opinions reveal a misunderstanding of the *"devout and active participation"* mandated by Vatican II.

"You Have Desecrated My Sabbath"

Is *"devout and active participation"* at Mass limited

to performing liturgical functions? No intelligent reading of the Second Vatican Council would support such an interpretation. In truth, the whole of revealed religion attests that liturgical participation is ordered to goodness and morality. The Old Testament prophets, for example, severely admonished the Israelites for attending temple worship while refusing to observe the Law of Moses. God severely laments the fact that the people have spurned what is holy and "have desecrated my Sabbath" (Ezekiel 23:8f; also Malachi 1:10-12). The prophet Jeremiah castigates the priests for not admonishing the people who, although they attended Sabbath worship, refused to repent and obstinately remained in their sins (see Jeremiah 2:1-8, 23:9-40; also Micah 3:1-12).

Yet, we know that persons in the state of mortal sin can benefit from attending Mass or even other sacraments such as penance or last anointing to the extent that they dispose themselves to receive the graces made available in the liturgy.

"Holy, Holy, Holy"

"*Devout and active participation by the faithful,*" the kind that God expects of His people, must begin with living in accord with the teachings of Christ as made known by His Holy Church. One must accept all the Church's faith and moral teachings.

"*Devout and active participation*" requires the practice of the beatitudes: kindness, gentleness and humility. At Mass, we should not only sing, "Holy, Holy, Holy." To offer "fitting" worship, we must seek to become "Holy, Holy, Holy." St. Peter said: "You are a chosen race, a royal priesthood, a holy nation, a redeemed people called to proclaim the glorious works of the One who brought you out of darkness into His marvelous light. Once you were not a people but now you are the People of God. Once there was no mercy for you. Now you have received mercy" (1 Peter 2:9-10).

The *Catechism of the Catholic Church* teaches that the Eucharist is called: "*Holy Mass* (Missa), because the liturgy, in which the mystery of salvation is accomplished, concludes with the sending forth (*missio*) of the faithful, so that they may fulfill God's will in their daily lives" (N. 1332). St. Paul concisely states what God expects from all of His children: "This is the will of God, your sanctification" (1 Thessalonians 4:3).

The Sacrifice Of The People

At the Offertory of the Mass, the priest prays: "Pray, brethren, that my sacrifice and yours may be acceptable to God, the Almighty Father." This supplication signifies that the priest and the faithful each uniquely participate in the one Sacrifice of Christ.

The priest offers the Eucharistic Sacrifice acting *in the Person of Christ*. He "makes present," perpetuates, Our Blessed Lord's redemptive sacrifice offered on Calvary.

What about the sacrifice of the people? The Second Vatican Council teaches that the faithful, "by reason of their baptism," offer spiritual sacrifice, one that is essentially different from that of the priest (see *Constitution on the Liturgy*, N. 48). The Council directs priests to: "(Instruct) their people to offer to God the Father the Divine Victim in the Sacrifice of the Mass and with Christ, the Divine Victim, make an offering of their whole lives" (*Decree on the Ministry & Life of Priests*, N. 5).

When the priest offers the Spotless Host to the Father, Our Lord desires that the people place their sacrifices and their crosses on the paten and unite them with His sufferings on the Cross. The people must place their sacrifices and their crosses on the paten and unite them with the sufferings of Our Blessed Lord. It is precisely at the Holy Sacrifice of the Mass that the "tears of life" take on infinite value.

In participating at Mass, we offer up our pain, suffering, loneliness, rejection, etc. Through Our Lord we offer these crosses to the Father, uniting them with the Sacrifice of Christ on the Cross of Calvary. This is *devout and active participation of the faithful*" in God's eyes. With St. Paul, we too can exclaim: "Now it is my joy to suffer for your sake. In my poor body, I make up what is lacking in the sufferings of Christ for the sake of His body which is the Church" (Colossians 1:24).

"At The Foot Of The Cross"

What a profound privilege it is to assist at the Holy Sacrifice! Truly, we are on Calvary "at the foot of the Cross with Mary, John and the Magdalene." The *Catechism of the Catholic Church* corroborates that our participation must be "in unity with the whole Church." Christ is the center of that unity. "To the offering of Christ are united not only the members still here on earth, but also those already in the glory of heaven. In communion with and commemorating the Blessed Virgin Mary and all the saints, the Church offers the Eucharistic Sacrifice. In the Eucharist the Church is, as it were, at the foot of the Cross with Mary, united with the offering and intercession of Christ" (N. 1370).

Viewing the Mass in this light, would we ever allow ourselves to "miss Mass?" Would we excuse ourselves by saying that we were on vacation or had to work? Indeed, would we let a single day go by without being at the foot of the Cross with Our Blessed Mother, St. John and St. Mary Magdalene?

Strengthened by Our Blessed Mother at Mass, we unite our sufferings with the redemptive agony of Christ crucified for the salvation of man! With St. Alphonsus de Liguori we pray: "We adore you, O Christ, and we praise you. Because by your Holy Cross, you have redeemed the world! Amen!"

"O! SACRED BANQUET!"

Upon entering the chapel of Christ the King Seminary, we seminarians recited, in Latin, the prayer of St. Francis of Assisi: "We adore You, Lord Jesus Christ, here and in every church throughout the world. We bless You because by Your Holy Cross You have redeemed the world." Then we added the profound prayer of St. Thomas Aquinas: "O! Sacred Banquet in which Christ is consumed, His Sacred Passion is remembered, the soul is filled with grace, and the pledge of future glory is given." To this day, whenever I come into the presence of the Blessed Sacrament, I recite these lovely prayers.

Jesus "Broke The Bread"

A banquet, according to Webster, is an "elaborate and often ceremonious meal for numerous people." When we receive Our Lord in Holy Communion, we feast on the Elaborate Meal; Jesus is truly our "Sacred Banquet." The Latin word for banquet that St. Thomas used was *convivium*. This word has the flavor of friends *joining together and becoming one* in the sharing of food, an absolute necessity for sustaining life. Thus, in the ancient East, breaking from the same loaf of bread was a sure sign of intimate friendship. Our Blessed Savior, on the night before He died "broke the bread and gave it to His disciples" (see *Catechism of the Catholic Church*, N. 1329). In the Holy Eucharist, Our Lord instituted the supreme gift of divine friendship between God and man.

However, Jesus does not merely share a banquet with us. *HE IS OUR CONVIVIUM, OUR BANQUET! HE IS OUR BREAD OF LIFE!* An absolute characteristic of love is that it always demands union. Our Blessed Lord, in His infinite love for every human person, wants to unite Himself with each of us in an unsurpassable intimacy, a supreme gift of divine friendship. What better gift could there be than His becoming our bread of life and our spiritual drink? Our Lord unites His Sacred Flesh with our flesh. His Precious Blood mingles with our blood! In Holy Communion, we "unite ourselves to Christ, who makes us sharers in His Body and Blood to form one single body" (*Catechism*, N. 1331).

We Share In Christ's Divinity

St. Paul tells us that members of Christ's Body share in "one Lord, one faith, one baptism" (Ephesians 4:5). The sacred banquet of the Eucharist is the source of that unity. At Mass, after pouring wine into the chalice, the priest adds a few drops of water. There is rich symbolism in this mingling. The Church teaches that the priest mixes water with wine "because it is believed that Christ did this and because from His side there came blood and water; the memory of this mixture is 'renewed' by this mixture, and since in the Apocalypse of St. John the "people" are called "waters," (17:1,15) and thus the union of the faithful with Christ their Head is represented" (Council of Trent, Session 22, Chapter 7).

At the Offertory of the Mass, the priest prays: "By the mystery of this water and wine, may we come to share in the divinity of Christ Who humbled Himself to share in our humanity." The drops of water represent us. St. Thomas Aquinas says: "We see that the people are signified by the water and Christ's blood by the wine. Therefore when water is mixed with the wine in the chalice, the people is made one with Christ" (*Summa Theologiae* III, q.74, a.6).

Our Divine Lord "humbled Himself to share in our humanity." At His invitation, "we come to share in the divinity of Christ." Imagine! We share in the divinity of Christ! Words fail us as we explore the Sacred Mysteries. The angels of the heavens wonder at the treasure that the

Father bestows upon His children on earth. Jesus, Our Divine Treasure, is the "Bread of Life." Like the centurion, we must humbly exclaim: "Lord! I am not worthy to receive You but only say the word and my soul shall be healed!"

His Sacred Passion Is Recalled

St. John Chrysostom makes this awe-inspiring observation: "When you see the Lord immolated and lying upon the altar, and the priest bent over the sacrifice praying, and all the people empurpled by that Precious Blood, can you think that you are still among men and on earth? Or are you not lifted up to heaven?"

When we receive Holy Communion, we are "empurpled by the Precious Blood." Like Mary Magdalene at the foot of the Cross, we are cleansed by the Blood of the Lamb. "Come now, let us set things right, says the Lord: Though your sins be like scarlet, they may become white as snow; though they be crimson red, they may become white as wool" (Isaiah 1:18).

The Soul Is Filled With Grace

"Without me you can do nothing," Jesus said (John 15:5). Man is endowed with a natural goodness. However, as members of His Mystical Body, Our Lord calls us to a supernatural goodness. How can we respond to this divine invitation in view of our fallen human nature?

"He who eats my flesh and drinks my blood has eternal life, and I will raise him up on the last day" (John 6:54). Our initiation into Catholic faith, began at Baptism and strengthened by the sacrament of Confirmation, comes to completion in the Eucharist. The Second Vatican Council teaches that the Eucharist is the "source and the summit of all the sacraments."(Cf. *Constitution on the Sacred Liturgy*, N. 10). Through the Holy Sacrifice of the Mass and the Blessed Sacrament, we receive the graces that we need to avoid sin and practice the virtues. Through the Eucharist and the other sacraments we receive the strength to carry out our vocations and live lives "worthy of the Gospel of Christ" (Philippians 1:27). Truly, the worthy reception of the sacraments and especially the Eucharist fills our souls with grace.

"Our Pledge Of Eternal Life"

The Holy Eucharist of Jesus is our pledge of eternal life. This pledge has been sealed in the Blood of the Lamb, the Lamb of God Who takes away the sins of the world. St. Augustine wrote: "O Sacrament of piety! O sign of unity! O bond of charity! Whoever wants to live, let him approach; let him believe; let him be incorporated so that he may live."

St. Thomas Aquinas extols the sacred mysteries profoundly in his marvelous hymn, *Panis Angelicus*:

> *The Bread of angels has become the Bread of mankind;*
> *This heavenly Bread puts an end to all images;*
> *O wonderful reality! The poor, the slave, and the*
> *humble eat the Lord.*

The "Bread of Angels" is God's *Gift Beyond Compare* that proclaims His infinite love for every human person. May the heart of Jesus, in the Most Blessed Sacrament, be praised adored and loved, with grateful affection at every moment, in all the tabernacles of the world, even to the end of time. Amen!

"WE ARE AMBASSADORS OF CHRIST!"

Every Holy Thursday the washing of feet takes place during the Chrism Mass. Pope Pius XII re-established this rite in the liturgy as a vivid reminder to Christ's faithful of Our Lord's humility. Jesus Christ is the Suffering Servant Who "came not to be served but to serve" (Mark 10:45).

However, the Holy Thursday liturgy is significant for reasons much more essential to our eternal salvation. On the night before He died Our Divine Savior offered the first Mass. He offered it in anticipation of the Sacrifice of His life on the Cross of Calvary. On Holy Thursday, Our Blessed Lord also instituted the Sacraments of the Eucharist and Holy Orders. The Eucharist is His Real Presence in sacrament and sacrifice. Holy Orders is the sacrament by which our Lord perpetuates His one priesthood until the end of time.

On the night that Our Blessed Lord was betrayed, "taking bread and giving thanks, he broke it and gave it to them saying, 'This is my body which is given for you. Do this in memory of me.' After supper, He took the cup, saying, 'This cup is the new covenant in my blood, which will be shed for you'" (Luke 22:19-20).

"Do this in memory of Me!" With those words, the first priests of the Roman Catholic Church were ordained. Peter, James, John, Andrew, Thomas and the other Apostles became "priests for all eternity." They came to share in the one Priesthood of Jesus Christ.

Who are these men, these priests of Jesus Christ? Pope Pius XII, in his Apostolic Exhortation *Menti Nostrae*, taught: "The priest is a 'second Christ.' Sealed with an indelible character, he becomes, as it were, a living image of the Savior." The Second Vatican Council teaches that, in the administration of the Sacred Mysteries, priests act, "in the very Person of Jesus Christ."

The preface of the Chrism Mass prays this penetrating portrayal of the priesthood: "(Jesus) appoints them to renew in His Name the sacrifice of our redemption as they set before (the Father's) family His Paschal Banquet. (Jesus) calls them to lead (the Father's) holy people in love, nourish them by (His) word, and strengthen them through the sacraments."

The Sacrifice Of Our Redemption

A priest is one who offers sacrifice to God in atonement for sin (see Hebrews 5:1-10). In offering the Holy Sacrifice of the Mass, the priest re-presents (makes present) Our Lord's Sacrifice on the Cross, offered for our redemption. The principal celebrant at every Mass is Jesus Christ, the Great High Priest and Our Divine Redeemer.

The Second Vatican Council teaches that the priest does not offer Mass as a representative of or even in place of Christ. NO! The priest offers Mass "IN PERSONA CHRISTI, in the very Person of Jesus Christ." When the priest says, "This is my Body. This is my Blood," he identifies, sacramentally, with Jesus Christ. Like the Great High Priest, who was both Priest and Victim on Calvary, the priest must also be priest and victim. Whatever crosses the Lord sends him, whatever sufferings he endures, the priest must unite them with the sufferings of the Divine Master. He also must be priest and victim.

What an exalted vocation! We priests share in the Priesthood of Jesus Christ! How humble this should make us! Pope Pius XII reminded us of this in *Menti Nostrae*: "Whatever he has or is comes from the goodness and the power of God. If he would glory, let him remember the words of the Apostle of the Gentiles: 'For myself I will glory in nothing but in my infirmities'" (2 Corinthians 12:5).

The Priest Strengthens God's People

The priest must strengthen God's people not only in the administration of the sacraments but through his priestly prayers. The Gospels frequently present us with Christ in prayer. Jesus "appointed twelve, to be with Him" (Mark 3:14). The Lord wants His priests with Him, always! In his unique identity with the Savior, the priest prays with Christ for his people. The faithful know this instinctively. Constantly, they seek the prayers of the priest for their spiritual and physical needs.

Pope John Paul II, in his 1987 Holy Thursday letter to priests, emphasizes that "our priesthood should be profoundly linked to prayer: rooted in prayer." Pius XII said that the priest should close his day by visiting the Blessed Sacrament. There, he adores Jesus and "makes amends for the ingratitude of men. He grows in divine love and finds his rest in the Sacred Heart of Jesus" (*Menti Nostrae*).

Pray For Priests

Reflecting on the Eucharist, the priest's intimate relationship with it becomes evident. The Eucharist is Christ with us. The priest is an *Alter Christus*, another Christ. As you kneel before the Blessed Sacrament, pray for vocations. We must have priests. Without the priest, we cannot have Jesus in the Eucharist. Without the priest, where will we find forgiveness for our sins? At the hour of death, the priest brings us the Sacraments of Penance, Holy Viaticum and Anointing. From the moment of our Baptism to the moment of death, the priest nourishes us with the word of God; he strengthens us with the Sacrifice of the Mass and the Sacraments.

We must also pray for priests since "(the priest) himself is beset with human weakness" (Hebrews 5:2). Our Lord "chooses the weak to confound the strong." In our human weakness, we priests carry the baggage of human frailty, baggage from which we would love to be released. With St. Paul, we cry out: "I delight in the law of God, but I see in my members another law at war with the law of my mind and making me captive to the law of sin" (Romans 7:22-23).

Despite our human weaknesses, show me an army of men that faithfully has carried the banner of Catholic truth down through the ages like the Priests of Jesus Christ! Peter said: "Depart from me Lord for I am a sinful man" (Luke 5:8). But the forgiving Savior did not depart from Peter. He raised him up from his human frailty and made him a fisher of men. This is our identity: we priests are fishers of men. The Catholic priest is ordained for the salvation and sanctification of souls. The priest of Jesus Christ is an *Alter Christus*! May God grant that we never forget it!

Mary, Our Blessed Mother, is the mother of priests in a special way. She strengthens us in our weakness, makes up for our failures and prays that we truly become "Ambassadors of Christ." Mary, Queen of the Clergy, pray for us!

"JESUS SAID TO HER: 'MARY !'"

It was a moving moment, one of the most moving in all of Sacred Scripture. "Mary stood beside the tomb, weeping" (John 20: 11). She struck the figure of a soul sheathed in an agony of sorrow. Her name was Mary, Mary Magdalene.

It was only a few months earlier, in the house of Simon the Pharisee, that she had anointed our Lord's sacred feet (see Luke 7:36-50). Now she would anoint His lifeless Body. But the tomb was empty! The Body of Jesus was gone. Who had taken It? Was It stolen? Had It been adequately anointed? Mary was in a frenzy!

Suddenly, a voice broke the early morning still: "Woman, why are you weeping? Who is it that you are looking for?" It was the Lord. In her anguished tears, however, she did not recognize Him. Thinking she had heard the voice of the gardener, she pleaded: "Sir, if you are the one who has carried him off, tell me where you have laid him and I will take him away" (John 20:15-16). Our Lord responded gently: "Mary!" In that electrifying moment, Mary Magdalene knew that it was Jesus!

A Woman Who Was A Sinner

Who was this Mary who expressed such intense love for Our Blessed Lord? Some Fathers of the Church believe that she was the sister of Martha and of Lazarus, whom Jesus had raised from the dead. They identify her with "the woman who was a sinner" (Luke 7:37). St. John tells us with certainty that Mary Magdalene was at the foot of the Cross with Our Blessed Mother and him (see John 19:25).

Lazarus and his sister Martha were dear friends of Our Lord. Devout Jews, they had faithfully followed the Law of Moses all their lives. However, Mary, their youngest sister, somehow went astray. In her youth, she had left home for the town of Magdala, located by the Sea of Galilee about five miles south of Capharnum. Because of its sunny shores, Magdala was the playground of the idle rich who flocked there in pursuit of pleasure. Casting aside her rich religious heritage, Mary plunged into the vices of this ancient city of sin with abandon. Soon, she became known as Mary of Magdala. St. Mark tells us that seven devils had taken hold of her (see Mark 16:9). Mary broke the hearts of Lazarus and Martha. Then one day she met the Lord. Perhaps it was a chance meeting. Perhaps, lost in her frenzied world of false loves and empty pleasures, she had sought Him out. The Gospels give no clue. When they met, His gentle but firm eyes looked into hers. It was a look that penetrated her tormented and sensitive soul, piercing her very being. Tears of repentance welled up in her eyes. Instantly, she became His disciple. Mary's heart had finally found the love that the world cannot give. Jesus, the Good Shepherd, had found His lost sheep. Never again would Mary leave Our Lord.

Jesus Appeared "*First* To Mary Magdalene"

It is interesting to note that St. Mark tells us that Our Blessed Savior "appeared *first* to Mary Magdalene, from whom he had cast out seven demons" (16:9). Pious Catholic belief, confirmed by private revelations to some saints, assures us that Our Lord first appeared to His own dear mother. What words could express the love that His Sacred Heart and her Immaculate Heart held for one another? Except for the three days loss, was she not with Him at every moment of His earthly sojourn? Does not Catholic faith confirm that she is the Mediatrix of the human race with her divine Son? (cf. *Lumen Gentium*, N. 62) Who would doubt that Our Lady's eyes were the first to see Him after His glorious resurrection?

Yet, Our Lord's first *recorded* appearance is to Mary Magdalene, the great sinner who became a great saint. It is in this way, I believe, that St. Mark confirms the mission of the Lord. His mission, the reason He was born, was the Redemption. He came to save the Magdalenes of this world. He came to save you and me. "The Son of Man has come to search out and save what was lost" (Luke 19:10). St. Paul says: "Make no mistake! Jesus Christ came into this world to save sinners" (1 Timothy 1:15). Mary, who was possessed by seven devils, repented. By the grace of Jesus Christ, she became a great saint. On Calvary, at the foot of the Cross, she represents each of us, the sinners of the world.

"Repent and believe in the Gospel," the Lord Jesus announced at the beginning of His public ministry (Mark 1:14). All of us have sinned. John, the beloved disciple, says that anyone who claims to be without sin is a liar (see 1 John 1:8).

Mary Magdalene is our model of repentance. Notice how art always portrays Mary kneeling at the foot of the Cross, her arms wrapped tightly around the Lord's feet. The Blood of the Lamb is pouring down on her head, literally washing away her sins. "Though your sins are like scarlet, they will become white as snow; crimson red, they will become white as wool" (Isaiah 1:18).

Our Model Of Eucharistic Devotion

Reflecting on this wonderful woman deepens our Eucharistic devotion. Every time we attend the Holy Sacrifice of the Mass, we are at the foot of the Cross with Mary, John and Mary Magdalene (see *Catechism of the Catholic Church*, N. 1370). On Good Friday, St. Mary Magdalene, with a heart filled with the love of Jesus, represented us sinners. Can we not say that she is with us at every Mass because we are a community of converted sinners? "In the Sacrifice-Banquet we hear the words of pardon, for the Eucharist is the visible sign of divine forgiveness" (Pius Parsch, *Year of Grace,* Vol. IV, p. 262).

St. Mary Magdalene is also our model of Eucharistic adoration. When Jesus called her by name she responded: "Rabboni." The scholars say that this word signifies Master. In this context, the word dons a nuance of great respect; it is a word which can be addressed to God Himself. Mary throws herself at the feet of Jesus. This is not an act of mere sentiment; Mary adored Our Risen Savior, Jesus Christ.

What devotion this marvelous saint must have displayed whenever a priest "Broke the Bread?" She understood the Holy Sacrifice of the Mass in a unique way. May this tremendous lover of the Lord teach us to love Jesus in the Holy Eucharist as she did. St. Mary Magdalene, pray for us sinners! May our repentance nourish our love for Our Blessed Lord and grow daily as did your great love for Him.

MY FAVORITE PRIEST

Notice that on the first Sunday after Easter, the Gospel narrates the institution of the Sacrament of Penance by Our Risen Lord. An intrinsic link binds together the Sacraments of the Eucharist, Penance and Holy Orders. The phrase "frequenting the sacraments" refers to the regular reception of the Sacraments of Confession and Communion. Neither sacrament can be had without the priest. The Catholic Church perpetuates the saving work of the Redemption through the Priesthood, the Holy Sacrifice of the Mass and the Seven Sacraments.

Catholics love their priests. Our "sense of Catholic faith," which we receive from Baptism and Confirmation, attests that the priest is an *Alter Christus*, another Christ. Think of the many priests that have affected our lives and have brought us closer to the Lord Jesus.

All Catholics have their favorite priests. Father John Mangon of the Annunciation Parish in Philadelphia came within minutes after we called him for Grandmom. To his dying day, Father Vincent Miceli was a fearless and unyielding defender of Catholic faith. Father William Heidt of Holy Apostles Seminary, Cromwell, CT has been a dear friend and confidant for years. Despite numerous trials and difficulties, Father Heidt has faithfully taught seminarians the truths of Catholicism for over fifty years.

These priests are outstanding examples of those who have been devoted to the Church and to their sacred calling. Truly, each one is an *Alter Christus*. My favorite priest, however, was the pastor of a small parish in northern Italy. Let me tell you about him.

Don Francesco Bellando

Several years after my ordination to the priesthood, I was living in Rome for continued studies. One day a call came to our residence from Bardonecchia, Italy. The pastor of San Ippolito's Parish, Don Francesco Bellando, needed a priest for Christmas. In responding to the call, I never suspected that I would spend every Christmas and Easter for the next four years at San Ippolito's as extraordinary confessor.

Bardonecchia is a picturesque skiing village near the French border. Vacationing tourists flock there from all parts of Italy. The shops are quaint and charming. Not even an austere saint could resist the luscious pastries of the bakeries. Anxious to breathe in the brisk Alpine air, vacationers swarm over the countryside. The church of San Ippolito dates to the eleventh century. A wall plaque lists a succession of pastors back to the year 1450.

Don Francesco was an engaging man and a priest to the core. As a young priest, he had received his doctorate in Canon Law. When he was appointed to Bardonecchia, it seemed to be the launching pad for a promising ecclesiastical career. Soon he was named a monsignor and often his name came up as a candidate for the episcopacy. But in the inscrutable designs of Almighty God, his star never rose. He remained the pastor of Bardonecchia for over fifty years until his death in 1992. "It matters not," he would muse. "Neither St. John Vianney nor St. John Bosco climbed the ecclesiastical ladder - - at least, not in this life."

His rectory was warm with priestly fraternity. Don Franco, his curate, was also a wonderful priest. Each evening I looked forward to the camaraderie that we enjoyed at table. The meals were simple but tasty. Always, there was plenty of pasta and vino!

"Always Remember The Mercy Of Jesus"

Don Francesco cautioned me that since many tourists came to town, one never knew what to expect when hearing confessions. "No matter what," the good priest insisted, "always remember that the mercy of Jesus Christ is without any limit and that He is most anxious to forgive. In this, we must ceaselessly reflect the Lord. Without exception, the priest must be seen as the friend of sinners." Don Francesco said that this is how he would like to be remembered, the "friend of sinners."

One evening at table, he remarked: "I always recall the words of Our Lord, 'I have not come to call the self-righteous but sinners.' How I wish that priests always would heed this divine demand of the Savior to administer His laws with mercy."

Not only was Don Francesco an exceptionally talented preacher but he also was filled with the love of Jesus Christ. "The priest," he would say, "should speak only of Jesus Christ, *La Madonna*, and of nothing else!" In a sermon, he once said: "Sure! Our Lord often spoke of things that people like to hear such as mercy, His forgiveness of sin, the love of one's neighbor and the like. However, Our Lord also spoke of things that many do not want to hear such as the observance of the Commandments, sin, and eternal separation from God in hell. The Lord did not speak of these things to terrorize us or to instill in us an unrealistic fear of God. No! He spoke of these things for our good. His greatest desire was to show us His divine mercy, if only we would seek it."

"This Is The Priesthood!"

Confessions were endless at Bardonecchia. We would begin at noon and often heard until midnight. One Christmas Eve, I finished at half past one in the morning, totally exhausted. Walking back to the rectory that cold December night, Don Francesco remarked: "Just think! The saintly Curé of Ars did this every day of his priestly life. This, caro Don Riccardo, is the priesthood!" He understood the priesthood. He knew that being a priest love with Our Lord in the Eucharist. This is how Don Francesco lived his vocation. This is how we, priests and laity, must live our vocations. We must love Jesus in the Blessed Eucharist.

In 1993, I received word from Don Franco that the Lord had called Don Francesco to Himself. But he was always with the Lord Jesus. He was with Him when He preached the Real Presence of Christ in the Eucharist. He was with Him when he offered the Holy Sacrifice of the Mass. He was with Him in his many, many visits to Jesus in the Blessed Sacrament.

Like his divine Master, dear Don Francesco Bellando gave us an example of priestly life. Truly, he was the "friend of sinners" who loved the Eucharistic Lord. Truly, he was an *Alter Christus*. May Our Blessed Mother, the Madonna who Don Francesco spoke of with such eloquence, teach us to love Jesus in the Most Blessed Sacrament of the Altar with an ever increasing love!

FORTY-HOURS DEVOTIONS AT BRAINARD

There was a time when practically every parish in the United States of America held Forty-Hours Devotions every year. This was a sure sign of the great devotion that Americans had for the Blessed Sacrament. In the last 25 years, however, this marvelous Eucharistic Devotion has practically disappeared. Thank God, a revival of Forty-Hours Devotions is taking place in some parishes. Holy Trinity Parish, Brainard, Nebraska, is one such parish. The pastor, Father Steven Cooney, graciously invited me to preach. My homiletic topics were *The Real Presence, The Sacrament of Penance* and *The Holy Sacrifice of the Mass*.

Devotions began with exposition of the Blessed Sacrament after the 10:30 Mass on Sunday. At least two adorers volunteered to "watch" with the Eucharistic Lord every hour. We closed the day with Benediction of the Blessed Sacrament. Exposition resumed after the 6:00 A.M. Mass the next day. During Benediction on the closing evening, Father Cooney carried the Blessed Sacrament under a canopy held by six men. The people came out from the pews and walked in procession. Young girls, dressed in white, scattered flower petals on the floor. The whole church was vibrant as the people joyously sang Eucharistic hymns. One could literally feel the Real Presence of the Lord Jesus. To add to the splendor, priests of the local deanery, vested in cassocks and surplices, were present.

It was glorious! The faith of the good people of Holy Trinity Parish was evident. About a hundred people from this small country parish attended the morning Masses. Many came during the day to adore the Lord Jesus enthroned in the monstrance. Each evening, the church was full for the evening devotions. The enthusiasm for this supreme spiritual event was obvious. From the pulpit, Father Cooney announced with joy that Forty-Hours would become an annual event. Our Blessed Lord, I am sure, will shower many blessings on His people at Brainard. For me personally, Forty-Hours Devotions at Holy Trinity Parish was a rich and rewarding experience.

Origins Of Forty-Hours

It is difficult to pinpoint the exact origins of Forty-Hours Devotions. Pope Clement VIII issued the Constitution *Graves et Diuturnae* on November 25, 1592. He ordered each parish of the 'Diocese of Rome to conduct a *Quarant' Ore*, forty hours of continuous adoration and prayer before the Blessed Sacrament. The main intentions were for the peace of the Universal Church and to combat the evils of the times. There is evidence that Forty-Hours Devotions existed in Milan, Italy in the twelfth century.

The format used was similar to today's. Solemn High Mass was followed by exposition of the Blessed Sacrament. The monstrance containing the Eucharist remained continuously enthroned on the main altar day and night. The closing ceremonies consisted of Benediction and a procession within the church and, when possible, outside.

When it was not practical to have all-night exposition, they reposed the Blessed Sacrament at the end of the day. The hours of adoration were then extended to the evening of the third day. The church was never to be without worshippers during this time. Churches were decorated magnificently and people came in crowds to hear the Word of God preached. The local priests faithfully attended. When devotions ended in one parish, they began in another. This ensured the continuous adoration of the Eucharist and that Forty-Hours Devotions always were being conducted at one of the Roman parishes.

After the Council of Trent, St. Charles Borromeo mandated that every parish of the Diocese of Milan must conduct Forty-Hours Devotions each year. The devotion spread throughout Europe and eventually to the United States, where it soon became an annual event at practically every parish. Devotion and respect for the Blessed Sacrament were without parallel here in America.

Devotion Diminishes

In the last 25 years, for some unexplained reason, Forty-Hours have practically disappeared. Because of this, I believe, devotion to the Eucharist has diminished. Faith in the Real Presence soon falters. This is evident from the frightful findings of the recent Gallup Polls which reveal that seventy percent of American Catholics no longer believe in the Real Presence of Our Lord in the Blessed Sacrament. More alarming, if that is possible, is that the doctrine of the Mass as the unbloody Sacrifice of Calvary is being obscured and often even denied.

Horror stories abound of desecrations and blasphemies committed against Our Eucharistic Lord. Dreadful liturgical abuses are inflicted upon the people under the guise of "meaningful liturgies." We must be ever vigilant against an indifferent attitude toward the Eucharist. The resurgence of Forty-Hours Devotions will ensure that our faith never grows cold or indifferent.

Eucharistic Reparation

One of the primary purposes of Forty-Hours Devotions is to make reparation for desecrations and indifference toward the Eucharist. Why not try to restore Forty-Hours Devotions in your parish? Perhaps a group could approach the pastor with this request. Blessings in abundance will come to you and to the parish from the Lord Jesus.

Perhaps your parish, or one close by, has perpetual adoration of the Eucharist. Why not sign up for an hour of adoration? Many people seek counseling these days. Seek out the Divine Counselor, Jesus Christ! Tell Our Blessed Lord that you believe in His Real Presence. Tell Him that you love Him. Bring your requests to the Eucharistic Lord. Like the blind man of the Gospels, simply say: "Jesus, Son of David, have pity on me." Jesus asked him what he wanted. "Lord," he pleaded, "that I may see!" The Compassionate Jesus responded without hesitation: "Receive your sight. Your faith has saved you" (Luke 18:35-43).

Your faith will save you, as well. Our Divine Savior, truly present in the Blessed Sacrament, will hear your prayers just as He heard the plea of the blind man of Jericho. His Sacred Heart, so familiar with sorrow, always responds to our desolate, human hearts. The Lonely Heart of Jesus awaits you in the Most Blessed Sacrament of the Altar. Do not disappoint Him!

"LOVELY LADY DRESSED IN BLUE!"

Mary! Mother! May! It is a marvelous month. Mothers are the most revered people on earth. They give us life. They nurse and nourish us. Mothers protect and guard us in a way that only they can. Most important of all, they love us. Our human hearts cannot survive without love; they were made for it. From the moment of conception, our mothers love us.

Archbishop Fulton J. Sheen once said that mothers were so wonderful that even God wanted one for Himself. God the Father chose Mary, the humble virgin of Nazareth, to give His Divine Son a human nature. On Calvary, Our Blessed Lord gave Mary to each of us, individually, to be Our Blessed Mother. The wonders of Catholic faith never cease as God showers His gifts upon us.

The Wedding Feast Of Cana

Reflecting on the Eucharist, let us meditate on Our Blessed Mother and the Gospel account of the wedding feast of Cana. What a marvelous story this is! Each new reading reveals another facet that previously escaped our eyes. At Cana in Galilee, Jesus performed the first of His miracles, the beloved disciple tells us (see John 2:1-11). Mary and His disciples were there and they witnessed what, indeed, turned out to be an extraordinary event. The Church, through the Liturgy of the Word, often proclaims a present-day reality by relating a past event. What happened at Cana centuries ago, happens now in a mystical, sacramental manner. At Cana, Our Blessed Lord changed water into wine. Now, at the Holy Sacrifice of the Mass, the Great High Priest changes wine into His Precious Blood. Through the power of His priest, who acts in *the Person of Jesus Christ*, the fruit of the vine becomes the Blood of Christ.

As he did at Cana, Our Blessed Lord keeps the choice Wine until last. He gives us the best of Wines; He gives us Himself! The Wine of His Precious Blood cheers our souls with His divine warmth. The Blood of Jesus becomes our spiritual drink!

"They Have No Wine!"

There is another important side of this tale that the Holy Spirit wants to keep ever before our eyes. The young wedding couple of Cana did not plan well. In the Eastern mind, the worst possible calamity is a lapse of hospitality. When faced with the dreadful situation of not having enough wine for the guests, the embarrassed newlyweds sought out Mary. In this they were wise for "never was it known that anyone who fled to her protection was left unaided!" Immediately, Our Lady told her Son of the couple's embarrassing situation.

The time for Our Lord to manifest Himself, however, was not at hand. Beginning His public ministry now was not within the Father's timetable. So, Our Lord said to his mother: "Woman, how does this concern of yours involve me? My hour has not yet come." Jesus' answer was definitely NO! It was not yet time to manifest His Messianic Mission!

A Mother's Prerogative

Faced with this dilemma, Our Blessed Mother did that which only a mother could do. She invoked her mother's prerogative. Turning to the waiters, she simply said: "Do whatever he tells you!" Not even the Lord can refuse His mother's insistence. Lest we forget, the Father can never refuse Our Lady's requests for she is the "apple of the Father's eye!" Because of her intercession, the schedule for the work of our Redemption was altered. Jesus changed water into the choicest of wines. Our Blessed Mother saved the day!

In his remarkable book, *Rendezvous With God*, Father Vincent Miceli laments how easily we forget to have recourse to Our Lady. "The trouble is we very often fail to appreciate and evaluate our friends. One of the most shamefully undervalued human friendships in all the world is between each one of us and the Mother of God. A perfect picture of how good a friend she is, is related by St. John in his story of the wedding feast of Cana. Were you to ask the host of that feast what he thought of Mary as a friend, he would tell you that she is the best friend he ever had in his life" (page 99). The Holy Spirit, through the Gospel of St. John, insured that the Church would always remember Our Lady's intervention.

At Cana, Peter, John and the other Apostles witnessed the intercessory power of the Mother of God! They learned a lesson that neither they nor the Church would forget until the end of time. May we never forget, in the words of St. Bernard, to "fly unto thee, O Virgin of virgins, my Mother."

In all our trials, in all the "tears of life," we fly to Our Blessed Mother. With a mother's heart, she hears us. She sees our hearts. Nothing escapes her mother's eye. She takes our needs to Our Lord and she says: "Son! They have no more wine!"

The marvelous Marian poem, "The Child on Her Knees" by Mary Dixon Thayer warms our hearts as we marvel at the mystery. In these tumultuous times, the Catholic heart needs to be warmed at times. We contemplate the Child being held in the arms of His mother, Mary. She is the Mother of God and she is Our Blessed Mother! Let us savor the words of the poetess:

Lovley Lady dressed in blue
Teach me how to pray
God was just your little boy
Tell me what to say!
Did you lift Him up, sometimes
Gently on your knee?
Did you sing to Him the way
Mother does to me
Did you hold His hand at night
And, did you ever try
Telling Him stories of the world?
And oh!, did He cry?
Do you really think He cares
If I tell Him things,
Little things that happen? and
Do angel's wings make a noise?
Can He hear me if I speak low?
Does He understand me now?
Tell me, for you know!
Lovely Lady dressed in blue
Teach me how to pray!
God was just your little boy
And you know the way!

"THE HIDDEN JESUS"

Mary, the Mother of God, appeared to three children at Fatima, Portugal on May 13, 1917. It was the first of six monthly apparitions to Lucia Santos, Francisco Marto and Jacinta Marto. On the day of the last vision, October 13, the sun literally danced in the heavens. Over a hundred thousand people witnessed this spectacular event which irrefutably confirmed that Our Blessed Mother really appeared. Pope Pius XII said that the revelations of Fatima were a "reaffirmation of the Gospels." Practically all of our Catholic beliefs, especially those concerning the Holy Eucharist, were confirmed at Fatima.

Three angelic appearances prepared the children for the vision of the Mother of God. The angel taught the young visionaries to make reparation to the Blessed Sacrament by prostrating themselves on the ground and praying: "O most Holy Trinity, Father, Son and Holy Spirit, I adore Thee profoundly. I offer Thee the Most Precious Body, Blood, Soul and Divinity of Jesus Christ, present in all the tabernacles of the world, in reparation for the outrages, sacrileges and indifference by which He is offended. By the infinite merits of the Sacred Heart of Jesus and the Immaculate Heart of Mary, I beg the conversion of poor sinners."

On his third visit, the angel held a chalice surmounted by a Host. "Take and receive the Body and Blood of Jesus Christ, horribly outraged by ungrateful men. Repair their crimes and console your God." An indescribable love for the Blessed Sacrament filled the hearts of the children. It was a love that would endure for the rest of their lives.

Lucia is still living and is a cloistered Carmelite nun in Portugal. As Our Lady predicted, Francisco and Jacinta died within a few years. Before dying, however, they grew to be giants in the spiritual life. Pope John Paul II has raised Francisco and Jacinta to the status of Venerable, the first official step toward sainthood. The Church is now praying for their canonization.

The Servant Of God, Francisco Marto

Francisco was a remarkable boy. He could only see Our Lady during the visions. For reasons known only to God and Our Lady, he could not hear her. Jacinta saw and heard. Only Lucia spoke to Our Lady. "Am I going to heaven?" Lucia asked on May 13.

"Yes, you are."

"And Jacinta?"

"Yes!"

"And Francisco?"

"He, too, but he must pray many Rosaries."

This baffling answer provokes our deep reflection. Are we doing all that we should to gain eternal salvation? Are we praying the Rosary as often as we should?

Charming stories abound about Venerable Francisco. One day three inquisitive ladies taxed him with the endless questions that all three of the children had to endure. Among other things, they asked what he wanted to be when he grew up.

"Do you want to be a carpenter?"

"No, madam."

"Surely you would like to be a doctor?"

"Not that either, madam."

"I know! You want to be a priest."

"No, madam."

"Well then," she exclaimed, "what do you want to be?"

"I don't want to be anything," Francisco said. "I just want to die and go to heaven. I want to be with the hidden Jesus." The "hidden Jesus" was Francisco's name for Jesus, truly present in the Blessed Sacrament.

Francisco's deep love for the Blessed Sacrament challenges our description. Our Blessed Mother had told him that he and his sister, Jacinta, would die soon. He was not frightened at all. Having seen Mary, life's wonders had no attraction for him. Often he skipped school. Inevitably he could be found kneeling before the Blessed Sacrament, talking to the hidden Jesus! "What does learning matter to me" he would say? "Soon, Our Lady will take me to heaven."

Shortly before Francisco's death, his parents sent for the priest. Before Father arrived, the dying boy asked his family: "I am going to confession now so that I can receive Holy Communion before I die. I want to know if you have seen me commit any sin." With heavy hearts, they pointed out his human peccadillos. Francisco's sensitive conscience urged him to be as pure as possible before receiving Jesus.

The priest placed the Sacred Host on his tongue. Francisco, now more angel than boy, received the Body of Christ with great reverence. Tears filled the eyes of all present. Alone with the hidden Jesus, Francisco was in an ecstasy of joy. Upon opening his eyes, he asked the priest: "When will you bring me the hidden Jesus again?" This was his only earthly desire. Our Lady, however, was about to come for him. Before the next day would dawn, Francisco Marto would be immersed in the eternal bliss of Heaven. The veils would be removed from the Blessed Sacrament. He was about to see Jesus, the One Whom we all long to see. He would see the Sacred Face of Jesus Christ! Francisco Marto was only ten years old.

Our Big Regret

The Poet once mused: "What fools these mortals be!" Yes! Think of the time we spend doing useless things. We spend hours watching television and doing other trivial things that will mean absolutely nothing in terms of eternity. Yet Jesus awaits us in the Blessed Sacrament. "Come to me, all you who labor and find life burdensome and I will refresh you" (Matthew 11:28). Hidden in the tabernacle, the Divine Counselor has the answer to every problem. He wipes away every tear and hears every plea. If only we would go to Him and empty out our hearts to Him.

Our Lord also waits for us to console Him for all the "outrages, sacrileges and indifference by which He is offended." But we are busy, too busy! I believe that on the Day of Judgment, we will all share one common regret. During our earthly sojourn, we were much too busy to visit the Blessed Sacrament. What excuse will we offer Our Lord when we face Him? Let us begin today to make regular visits to the "hidden Jesus." Venerable Francisco, pray for us! Teach us to love Jesus in the most Blessed Sacrament.

FIVE FIRST SATURDAYS

As Our Blessed Mother foretold, she took Francisco and Jacinta Marto to Heaven soon after her apparition at Fatima. She came for Jacinta on February 24, 1920. Like Lucia and Francisco, Jacinta had a deep love for Our Lord in the Blessed Sacrament.

Jacinta longed to be near the "hidden Jesus." When possible, Lucia went to daily Mass and Holy Communion. She always visited Jacinta on her way home from Mass. "Lucia, you have just been to Holy Communion," the dying child would say. "Please come and sit close to me because you have the hidden Jesus inside of you." Our Lady had taught Jacinta to love Jesus in the Blessed Sacrament. Since she was Mary's personal student, her devotion knew no limits.

Our Lady taught Jacinta many other lessons. She revealed to her that the Holy Father would have to suffer much. Lucia has told us of Jacinta's vision of the Holy Father. Jacinta saw him weeping while he was deep in prayer. Whenever Jacinta said the rosary, she added three Hail Marys for the Holy Father.

The July 13 Apparition

Jacinta had a burning desire for the conversion of sinners. This was a direct result of the July 13, 1917 apparition. On that day, Our Lady opened her arms. Suddenly, a ray came forth which seemed to pierce the earth. Before their eyes was a vision of Hell! In all its horror, it was dreadful beyond description. Lucia says that their terror was such that they would have died instantly had not Our Blessed Mother sustained them.

Prayer, penance and the conversion of sinners are at the heart of the Fatima message. Our Lady asked the children to pray many Rosaries for the conversion of sinners.

She also said that she wanted "Communions of Reparation" to be made on the first Saturday of each month.

On December 10, 1925, Our Lady appeared again to Sister Lucia, then a Dorothian nun. The Child Jesus was at her side. In one hand she held out a heart surrounded by thorns and said: "My daughter, look at my heart surrounded with thorns. Ungrateful men pierce it at every moment by their blasphemies and ingratitude. You, at least, try to console me. Tell them that I promise to assist at the hour of death, with all of the graces necessary for salvation, all who go to confession and Holy Communion on five consecutive first Saturdays. They must also recite five decades of the Rosary and keep me company for fifteen minutes while meditating on the mysteries of the Rosary with the intention of making reparation to me" (See *Fatima Today*, by Father Robert Fox, page 217).

The importance of the First Saturday Devotions cannot be overstated. By complying with our Blessed Mother's request, we can make reparation for our own sins and the sins of others. Modern society is deeply wounded by sin and its consequences. Scores of families are plagued by disharmony and destruction. Devout parents have made great sacrifices to raise their children in the Catholic Faith. Yet many young people have fallen away, causing their parents pain and anxiety. I know many such couples. They bring their crosses to Our Lady, faithfully making their Saturday "Communions of Reparation." They pray the Rosary every day, as Mary asked. Who could doubt that this good Mother in Heaven will answer their prayers?

Mary's Promise

Think of it! By complying with the First Saturday conditions, we have the Mother of God's personal guarantee that she will be with us at the hour of our death with all of the graces necessary for salvation. Father Fox makes this ardent plea in his book, *Fatima Today*: "Do we want peace? Do we want to save the souls of poor sinners who would otherwise go to Hell? Do we want to save the world from punishment by means of war, hunger, and the persecution of the Church and the Holy Father? Do we want the conversion of Russia? Then we must make the First Saturdays in reparation to Mary's Heart. Most certainly we all want the bonus, the graces necessary for our own salvation at the hour of death" (page 222).

"In the end," Our Blessed Lady said at Fatima, "my Immaculate Heart will triumph." We must trust her! The words of her divine Son, hanging from the Cross of Calvary, never escape her: "Woman! Behold your son!" In that moment of agony, she gave birth to each of us in the order of grace. Standing by the Cross on Calvary, she became Our Blessed Mother and the Mother of Mercy. In heaven, she never ceases to plead for us.

At Fatima, the angel taught the children to say this prayer at the end of each decade of the Rosary. "O my Jesus, forgive us our sins. Save us from the fires of Hell. Lead all souls to Heaven, especially those most in need of thy mercy." Have you made the Five First Saturdays as Our Lady asked? Are you making the "Saturday Communions" of Eucharistic reparation for your own sins and the sins of others? Mary wants us to grow in love for her Son in the Most Blessed Sacrament. This First Saturday is the best time to start. Don't disappoint Our Blessed Mother!

"I AM THE LADY OF THE ROSARY!"

At Lourdes the Blessed Virgin Mary identified herself to Bernadette Soubirous by saying: "I am the Immaculate Conception." This awe-inspiring title is rich in theological meaning. However, young Bernadette simply did not understand the meaning of these words. For centuries the Fathers and Doctors of the Church have reflected upon this unique privilege of Our Lady. In 1854 Pope Pius IX defined the Immaculate Conception of the Blessed Virgin Mary as an article of Catholic faith.

At Fatima Mary identified herself simply by saying: "I am the Lady of the Rosary." Everyone immediately understood this lovely title. The Rosary is the most popular of Catholic prayers. St. Dominic received the Rosary from the hands of the Mother of God herself. She inspired him to spread this devotion throughout the world. Let us now reflect on the Rosary and its link to the Most Holy Eucharist.

The Rosary Is A Gospel Prayer

In 1974 Pope Paul VI wrote the Apostolic Exhortation *Marialis Cultus*, Devotion to the Blessed Virgin Mary. In this document, the Holy Father exhorted the faithful to pray the Rosary. He stressed the teaching of Pope Pius XII, who said that the Rosary was a "compendium of the entire Gospel."

In *Marialis Cultus,* Paul VI was clear: "As a Gospel prayer, centered on the mystery of the Redemptive Incarnation, the Rosary is a prayer with a clearly Christological orientation." In other words, the Rosary's main focus is Jesus Christ and His saving mission of the Redemption.

The Rosary And The Mass

The Rosary is a devotion that easily harmonizes with the liturgy. Pope Paul said: "The Rosary is an exercise of piety that draws its motivating force from the liturgy and leads naturally back to it, if practiced in conformity with its original inspiration. In fact, meditation on the mysteries of the Rosary, by familiarizing the hearts and minds of the faithful with the mysteries of Christ, can be an excellent preparation for the celebration of those same mysteries in the liturgical action and can also become a continuing echo of it" (N. 48).

Praying the Rosary, therefore, is a wonderful way to prepare for Mass and the worthy reception of Holy Communion. The Rosary is an excellent prayer to say during holy hours and various private devotions. With Our Lady, we can meditate on the significance of the Eucharistic mysteries throughout the day.

The School Of Mary

The Rosary is a completely Catholic prayer. We begin with the Apostle's Creed, which affirms our allegiance to the Catholic Church. Then we attend the School of Mary and contemplate the reality of the Gospel events. Mary, the supreme catechist, reveals the wealth of Catholic faith to us for "she treasured all these things and reflected on them in her heart" (Luke 2:19).

The Joyful Mysteries focus on the coming of the Messiah and the unique role of Our Lady in the work of Redemption. The Sorrowful Mysteries recall Our Blessed Lord's Passion and Death. The Glorious Mysteries bring the saving work of Jesus to its inevitable triumph over sin, Satan and eternal death. We conclude in jubilation with the whole heavenly court by proclaiming Our Blessed Mother to be the Queen of Heaven and Earth.

As a child, I learned Catholic faith from my grandmother who raised me. Maria Rego was an immigrant from Naples who had no formal education at all. Yet, she knew her faith well. Every evening at 8:00, without fail, she prayed her Rosary. She would tell me about the birth of Jesus, His life and finally, His death on the Cross.

Saturday was *"La Madonna's"* special day. Every Saturday morning Grandmom took me to the Annunciation Church in South Philadelphia for Mass. It was Grandmom who first taught me about the Blessed Sacrament. I remember her pointing to the tabernacle and telling me that Jesus was inside. She did not learn the truths of these mysteries from books. Grandmom learned these things from praying her Rosary. The rich meaning of these sacred mysteries focus our attention on the Eucharistic Sacrifice and Sacrament. My grandmother was a student of Our Lady. She attended the School of Mary and she took me with her.

"Sweetens The Soul Like A Song"

Pope Paul VI said in *Marialis Cultus* that the Rosary is "lyrical and full of praise during the tranquil succession of Hail Marys." Pope John Paul I, who was with us for such a short time, said that repetition of the *Ave Maria* during the Rosary "sweetens the soul like a song."

The Hail Mary is an unending song of praise of Jesus Christ. St. Paul said that at the Name of Jesus, every knee must bend in heaven and on earth (see Philippians 2:10). According to St. Peter, it is only through the Name of Jesus that we are saved (see Acts 4:12). In adoration, we bow our heads at the Holy Name of Jesus with each Hail Mary.

Mother Of God!

What a profound expression! MOTHER OF GOD! How can a mere mortal be the Mother of God? Yet, Mary is the Mother of God! The Church teaches that Our Lord is

True God and True Man. His Human Nature, which He received from Mary, is hypostatically united to His Divine Person. Therefore, St. Cyril of Alexandria insisted that we must call Mary the Mother of God!

Today, many so-called scholars deny the divinity of Jesus. You can be sure that they never pray the Hail Mary. Every time we say "Mother of God" we affirm that Jesus Christ is divine! He is the Son of God! He is our Lord and Savior! Is it any wonder that many of these "scholars" discourage the recitation of the Rosary?

Mother Of Mercy

When we pray the Hail Mary, we ask Our Blessed Mother to "pray for us sinners." This simple phrase is a constant reminder of our sinfulness. Our Blessed Mother is reminding us of our need for the Sacrament of Penance. St. John is clear: "If we say, 'we are free of the guilt of sin,' we deceive ourselves; the truth is not in us" (1 John 1:8).

As repentant sinners, let us appeal to Mary. She is the Mother of Mercy, the Refuge of Sinners and the Gate of Heaven. St. Alphonsus de Liguori assures us that anyone who has true devotion to Our Blessed Mother can be assured of eternal salvation.

Dear Blessed Mother, guide us on our way to heaven. We want to be with Jesus. We want to be with you. We want to be with St. Joseph and the angels and saints, forever. Teach us to love Jesus, your Divine Son, in the Most Blessed Sacrament. You are Our Lady of the Most Blessed Sacrament! Amen!

THE LAUDA SION
(Part One)

Pope John XXIII, in his encyclical letter *Mater et Magistra*, identified the Church as *Mother and Teacher*. He writes: "The Church is the Mother and Teacher of all nations. She was such in the mind of her Founder, Jesus Christ. The Church holds the world in an embrace of love. Men in every age should find in her their ultimate completeness in a higher order of living and their ultimate salvation. She is the 'pillar and the bulwark of truth' (N. 1). Man's "ultimate salvation," of course, is eternal happiness with God in Heaven.

In every age, the Roman Catholic Church gives witness to Jesus and His redemptive death on the Cross of Calvary. "You will receive power when the Holy Spirit comes," Jesus commanded the Apostles, "and you will give witness to me in Jerusalem, throughout Judea and Samaria, and to the ends of the earth" (Acts 1:8).

Through the liturgy of the Mass, the Church prays what she believes. The Mass Orations, the Liturgy of the Word and the Eucharistic Prayers are chock full of doctrinal and moral truths. The Solemnity of *Corpus Christi* - - of the Body of Christ - - is a good example of the Catholic Church teaching us through the Holy Sacrifice of the Mass.

The Solemnity of *Corpus Christi* originated in Belgium in the thirteenth century. In 1264 Pope Urban IV extended the celebration to the Universal Church. He commissioned the Dominican, Thomas Aquinas, to write the liturgical office for the feast. St. Thomas composed the *Lauda Sion, Pange Lingua, Panis Angelicus* and the *Verbum Supernum*. These hymns are masterpieces of Eucharistic doctrine and adoration. The *Lauda Sion* is the Sequence of the Mass of *Corpus Christi*. In this meditation, let us savor its rich fare of Eucharistic doctrine and devotion emanating from the very soul of the Angelic Doctor.

Drawing from the writings of St. Augustine, the Second Vatican Council refers to the Eucharist as the *Paschal Banquet*. St. Thomas teaches us this in *Lauda Sion*: "At this table of the new King, the new law's new Pasch puts an end to the old Pasch. The new displaces the old, reality the shadow and light the darkness." What does St. Thomas mean by the "old Pasch" and the "new Pasch?" For the answer, we must reflect on the Sacred Scriptures.

The "Old Pasch"

Moses stood before Pharaoh and said: "Thus says the Lord, 'Let my people go so that they may worship me!'" Repeatedly, Moses made this demand of the Pharaoh; but Pharaoh remained obstinate. God then visited nine plagues upon the Egyptians. Yet, these severe punishments did not soften the hardness of the Pharaoh's heart; he refused to comply with God's demand. Moses then made his final appeal. If the Pharaoh continued to disobey God, the first-born of every Egyptian family would be struck dead, from the Pharaoh to the first-born of the least slave girl, and the animals as well. Still, Pharaoh refused! In punishment, God sent the angel of death! The Israelites, however, he spared from this scourge.

God instituted the Passover meal as the memorial of His delivering the Israelites from bondage to the Egyptians. This is how it was to be observed. Every family was to obtain a year-old lamb, without blemish. They were to slaughter it and apply some of its blood to the door posts of every house where the lamb was eaten. "This is how you are to eat it: with your loins girt, sandals on your feet and your staff in hand, you shall eat like those who are in flight. It is the Passover of the Lord. For on this night, I will go through Egypt, striking down every firstborn of the land, both man and beast, and executing judgment on all the gods of Egypt, I, the Lord! But the blood will mark the houses where you are. Seeing the blood, I will pass over you; thus, when I strike the land of Egypt, no destructive blow will come upon you" (Exodus 12:11-13).

This was the Passover meal of the Old Covenant, the "old Pasch" to which St. Thomas referred. The word Pasch itself means passage. Thus, the Passover Meal commemorated the "passage" of the Israelites from bondage to Pharaoh and slavery to the Egyptians. The "old Pasch" also memorialized the night that God delivered the Israelites from the punishment exacted by the angel of death.

The "New Pasch"

On Holy Thursday night, Our Blessed Lord instituted the "new Pasch." Jesus Himself is the Paschal Lamb Who is sacrificed "for us men and for our salvation." Our Blessed Lord is the Passover of our salvation. Just as the Old Covenant was a preparation for the New Covenant, the "old Pasch" prefigures the new (see Discourse of Pope John Paul II, April 13, 1995).

At the Last Supper, Our Divine Savior said to the Apostles: "I have greatly desired to eat *THIS PASSOVER* with you before I suffer" (Luke 22:15). "This Passover" refers to this new Passover that the Redeemer was about to offer up to the Father. Jesus Christ established the New Covenant sealed in His Blood. The Old Covenant was replaced by the New Covenant which is the Church. The Passover Banquet of the New Testament took the place of the Passover meal of the Old Testament. Jesus Christ Himself is the "lamb without blemish." Jesus Christ is the "Lamb of God who takes away the sin of the world" (John 1:29).

When Our Blessed Lord said: "This is my Body; this is my Blood," He offered, in an unbloody manner, the same sacrifice that He would offer on Calvary in a bloody manner. The "old Pasch" memorialized the deliverance of the Israelites. The "new Pasch," the Holy Eucharist, is the re-presentation of the Sacrifice of Calvary. Jesus redeemed mankind from the bondage to Satan, the slavery to sin and the punishment of death, eternal death. The Catholic Church, the Mystical Body of Christ, is the new Israel, the new People of God.

St. Thomas says: "(The Eucharist) has the nature of a sacrifice inasmuch as it is offered up; it has the nature of a sacrament inasmuch as it is received" (*Summa* III, Q. 79, A. 5). In the Holy Sacrifice of the Mass, Our Lord is both Priest and Victim. In the Blessed Sacrament, Jesus Christ is our Paschal Banquet. "At this table of the new King, the new law's new Pasch puts an end to the old Pasch. The new displaces the old, reality the shadow and light the darkness. Christ wanted what He did at the supper to be repeated in His memory."

The wonders of the Eucharistic mystery never cease. The more we explore them, the more we marvel. Jesus Christ is Our Eucharistic Lord. Jesus Christ is the Tremendous Lover of Man. Humbly, we can only repeat the words of the centurion, "Lord! I am not worthy that thou should come under my roof. But only say the word and my soul shall be healed" (Matthew 8:8).

LAUDA SION
(Part Two)

As we have observed, the Church constantly teaches us through the liturgy. Let us now examine a few more teachings of St. Thomas Aquinas in the hymn *Lauda Sion*, which is the Mass Sequence for the Solemnity of *Corpus Christi*.

"A Lively Faith"
In this magnificent hymn, St. Thomas insists on the necessity of "a lively faith" in the Real Presence. "Man cannot understand the Eucharist. He cannot perceive it. A lively faith, however, affirms that the change, which is outside the natural course of things, takes place. Under the different species, which are now signs only and not their own reality, there lie hid the wonderful reality. His Body is our Food, His Blood our Drink."

Our senses discover only bread and wine when they perceive the Sacred Species. They fail to perceive the reality of Christ's Presence. We see, feel, taste and smell bread and wine, nothing else. Nevertheless, we believe that Jesus is truly present! In his hymn *Adoro Te Devote*, St. Thomas says: "Because of the word of Jesus, we believe."

The key word here is "believe." Although Our Lord often revealed His divine power, He never gave us empirical proof that His Flesh and Blood are real Food and Drink. If He had done so, we could never practice the virtue of faith. Jesus wants our faith; He will accept nothing less (see John 6:68).

Faith does not mean that one understands. In truth, we simply do not understand! If we understood the mystery of the Eucharist, there would be no mystery at all. Years ago I was giving instructions to a very devout Protestant lady. She sincerely wanted to embrace Catholicism but she said that she "had a problem with the Eucharist." She said that she could not understand it. I told her that Our Lord never sought our understanding. He insisted on faith.

After some thought, she said that since Jesus wanted faith, she would give it to Him. With great joy, I received her into the Roman Catholic Church. Belief in the Eucharist is at the heart of our holy religion. With St. Thomas we affirm: "His Body is our Food, His Blood our Drink."

"Christ Remains Entire"

The Church teaches that the whole Christ, Body, Blood, Soul and Divinity, is present under each separate species. This is known as the Doctrine of Concomitance. The *Lauda Sion* attests that: "Christ remains entire under each species. The communicant receives the complete Christ, uncut, unbroken and undivided."

Now that it is permitted for all Christ's faithful to receive Holy Communion under both species, it is important to be aware of this doctrine. When one receives the Sacred Host, one receives the whole Christ, Body, Blood, Soul and Divinity. When one receives the Precious Blood, one receives the whole Christ, Body, Blood, Soul and Divinity.

"The Good And The Wicked Receive"

St. Thomas is very straightforward concerning worthy reception. "The good and the wicked alike receive Him, but with the unlike destiny of life or death. To the wicked it is death, but life to the good. See how different is the result, though each receives the same."

These words of the saint may seem harsh in these days of political correctness and permissive psycho-prattle. Yet St. Paul is equally clear. Writing under the inspiration of the Holy Spirit, he insists: "Whoever eats the bread or drinks the cup of the Lord unworthily sins against the body and blood of the Lord. A man should examine himself first. Only then should he eat of the bread and drink of the cup. He who eats and drinks unworthily, eats and drinks judgment to himself for not having discerned the body of the Lord" (1 Corinthians 11:27-29).

This teaching was clear to everyone a few decades ago. Now, it has become obscure in the minds of many. Whatever the reason may be for this serious lapse, we must heed the teachings of the Church. In order to receive the Eucharist *worthily*, one must be morally certain that he is free of mortal sin. A person who is conscious of having committed a mortal sin must confess it in the Sacrament of Confession before receiving Holy Communion. Simply making an Act of Contrition, without prior confession, does not suffice.

Let us remember that, in the Eucharist, Jesus wants to unite us to Himself. St. Thomas says that when we receive Holy Communion, "(we) are made one with Christ . . . and are being prepared to enter into everlasting life" (see *Summa Theologiae* III, Q 74, A 6). Before uniting ourselves with the Divine Lord, we must cleanse ourselves from mortal sin. If we fail to do so, we must not receive so sublime a sacrament.

"They Have Washed Their Robes!"

"Every time you eat this bread and drink this cup," St. Paul says, "you proclaim the death of the Lord until he comes in glory" (1 Corinthians 11:26). When our Lord comes again in glory, every human being will rise from the dead. Everyone, without exception, will be reunited with their bodies (see 1 Corinthians 15:51-57). Jesus, the King of Glory "will judge the living and the dead." Our Divine Savior will complete His work of redemption by handing over to the Father the New Israel, the Church Triumphant.

Jesus will unite His beloved disciples with Himself for all eternity. "These are the ones who have survived the great period of trial; they have washed their robes and made them white in the Blood of the Lamb" (Revelation 7:14).

During their lives, these blessed of the Lord have washed their robes and made them white in the great Sacraments of Baptism and Holy Confession. They have been nourished by the Body and Blood of Our Merciful Savior, Jesus Christ. They have adored Him at the Holy Sacrifice of the Mass and in the Most Blessed Sacrament. God grant that each of us will "survive the great period of trial." In the words of St. Ignatius Loyola we cry out:

"Soul of Christ, sanctify me;
Body of Christ, save me;
Blood of Christ, inebriate me;
Water from the side of Christ; wash me;
Passion of Christ, strengthen me!" *Amen!*

THE LAUDA SION
(Part Three)

Down the centuries, St. Thomas Aquinas has enriched every Catholic with the treasure of his wisdom and devotion. The lovely lyrics of his Eucharistic hymn, *Tantum Ergo*, are a constant inspiration during Benediction of the Blessed Sacrament. "Humbly let us voice our adoration for so great a sacrament. Let all former rites surrender to the Lord's New Testament. Faith replaces what our senses fail to see. Glory, honor and adoration, let us sing out with one accord. Praised be God, the Almighty Father. Praised be Jesus Christ, His Son, Our Lord. Praised be God the Holy Spirit, Triune Godhead be adored! Amen!"

"As Much In A Fragment"
Let us return to our analysis of the *Lauda Sion*. The Angelic Doctor teaches us that Jesus is truly present in every particle of the Sacred Host. "If the sacrament is broken, have no doubt," St. Thomas instructs us. "Remember there is as much in a fragment as in an unbroken host."

This doctrine of the Church is extremely important. Many persons have been commissioned as extraordinary ministers of the Eucharist. Every visible particle contains the Real Presence of Jesus. This principle holds true no matter how small the particle. Notice how carefully priests purify the sacred vessels after the Communion of the Mass. He must be careful to consume every visible fragment.

Obviously, everyone must take every reasonable precaution when handling the Blessed Sacrament. Recall that the Lord prepared the Apostles for this when He "broke the seven loaves for four thousand." Our Lord wanted to know how many fragments they had collected from what remained (see Mark 8:20).

Our Lord, Jesus entrusts Himself to us in the

Eucharist. Lovingly aware of His Divine Presence, we must be vigilant that every "fragment be collected."

"The Pilgrim's Food"

The *Lauda Sion* continues: "Behold, the bread of angels is become the pilgrim's food; truly it is bread for sons and is not to be cast to dogs. It was prefigured in type when Isaac was brought for an offering, when a lamb was appointed for the Pasch and when manna was given to the Jews of old."

The Second Vatican Council teaches us that we are a "pilgrim people" on our journey to eternal life. The Eucharist is the Bread of Angels that sustains us along the way. How could we find our way to God without the spiritual nourishment of the Holy Eucharist? How could we resist the temptations of the world, the flesh and the devil without the indispensable graces that we receive in Holy Communion? "Without me," Our Blessed Lord said, "you can do nothing" (John 15:5).

Pope John Paul II, in his Wednesday Audience of April 12, 1995, said that the Eucharist must be the central focus of our lives. "The mysterious reality of the Eucharist *introduces believers into the 'plan' of God, Creator and Redeemer.* God wanted His only Son to be incarnate and ever present among us as our traveling companion on the arduous journey toward Heaven."

The Holy Father's words inspire us to receive Holy Communion often, even daily. Imagine! In the Eucharist, the Son of God is our traveling companion on our journey of life. In his address, the Pope reminds us that the Eucharist is the source of strength by which we remain faithful to every vocation. "It must be at the heart of the life of priests and consecrated people. It must be the light and strength of spouses in putting into practice their commitment to fidelity, chastity and the apostolate. Jesus in the

Eucharist is the ideal in education and in training children, adolescents and young people. Our Eucharistic Lord is the comfort and support of those who are troubled, of the sick and all who are weeping in the Gethsemane of life. He must be for everyone the incentive to fulfill the testament of divine charity in humble and joyous availability to our brothers and sisters, as the Lord taught by His own example, washing the Apostles' feet."

Our Blessed Lord said: "I am the Bread of life." How pitiable are those who seldom, if ever, receive Holy Communion! They are the poorest of the poor, the most desolate of the desolate because they are spiritually starving to death. How can we possibly endure the "Gethsemane of life" without the strength we receive from the Eucharist? Jesus is the "Bread of Angels," St. Thomas tells us, Who has "become the pilgrim's food."

"Have Mercy On Us!"

The pagan world, in its mad rush to explain away the concrete reality of sin, has forgotten our common need for God's mercy. Because of our many sins, we desperately need divine mercy. In his encyclical letter *Dives in Misericordia*, Pope John Paul II teaches us about God's mercy: "In Christ and through Christ, God becomes especially visible in His mercy; that is to say, there is emphasized that attribute of the divinity which the Old Testament, using various concepts and terms, already defined as 'mercy.' Christ confers on the whole of the Old Testament tradition a definite meaning about God's mercy. Not only does He speak of it and explain it by the use of comparisons and parables, but above all *He Himself makes it incarnate and personifies it. He Himself, in a certain sense, is mercy.* To the person who sees it in Him, and finds it in Him, God becomes 'visible' in a particular way as the Father "who is rich in mercy" (N. 2).

Let us kneel before Our Lord in the Blessed Sacrament and humbly seek His mercy. Like the tax collector who would not dare "to raise his eyes to heaven," let us cry out from the depth of our human weakness: "O God! Be merciful to me, a sinner" (Luke 18:13)! This is a plea that Jesus, the Good Shepherd, cannot resist. Our Blessed Lord will hear our plea just as He hears everyone who seeks His mercy. Jesus Christ, the Redeemer of Man, will come to you with every grace. He will enrich your life with His gentle goodness. He will grant you with the grace to become holy.

Jesus, the Merciful Savior, forgave the woman caught in adultery and the Samaritan woman who had five husbands. To Zacchaeus, the tax collector, Our Lord said: "Today salvation has come to your house, for this is what it means to be a son of Abraham. The Son of Man has come to search out and save what was lost" (Luke 19:9-10).

In His Infinite Mercy, Our Divine Savior raised Mary Magdalene from the pitiable state of a shocking sinner to the lofty status of a great saint. His mercy changed Peter, the sinner (see Luke 5:8) to Peter, the Fisherman. Saul of Tarsus was the "chief of sinners" (see 1 Timothy 1:15). Yet, the grace of Jesus Christ enabled Saul, the Persecutor, to become St. Paul, the Apostle of the Gentiles. The mercy of Jesus Christ is the constant theme of the New Testament. St. Luke's Gospel, often called the Gospel of Mercy, abounds with stories of mercy.

In the *Lauda Sion*, St. Thomas pleads with the Eucharistic Lord for mercy. May his prayer be ours: "Jesus, Good Shepherd and True Bread, have mercy on us; feed us and guard us. Grant that we find happiness in the land of the living. You know all things and can do all things. You feed us here on earth. Make us citizens in Heaven, co-heirs with You and companions of Heaven's citizens. Amen. Alleluia."

ST. MARIA GORETTI, PATRONESS OF YOUTH

The Catholic Church recognizes the fact that every young person can attain a very high degree of holiness. Note the ages of a few saints canonized in our century. St. Bernadette was thirty-five when she died. St. Therese of Lisieux was twenty-five. St. Dominic Savio, a pupil of St. John Bosco, was only fifteen. His motto was: "Death rather than sin." The Servants of God, Jacinta and Francisco Marto, were nine and ten years old. All of these young people had a deep love and devotion for Our Lord in the Blessed Sacrament.

This is certainly true of St. Maria Goretti who is the subject of this Eucharistic reflection. Young Maria was twelve years old when she gave her life defending her purity. The Church has placed her feast day in the liturgical calendar on July 6.

Maria's Love For The Eucharist

Born in 1890, Maria Goretti lived with her family on a small farm near Nettuno, Italy. Early in her life, she formed the habit of frequent Confession and Communion. Maria showed her respect for the Blessed Sacrament on the day of her First Holy Communion. After Mass, she heard a classmate tell an indecent joke. Appalled, she said: "How could you so soon forget Jesus? I would rather die than talk of such things." St. Paul says: "Sexual immorality and lust of any kind must not be even mentioned among you! It offends your holiness" (Ephesians 5:3).

"No! No! It Is A Sin!"

Maria looked forward to a quiet life of marriage and children. Nothing suggested the great trial that awaited her or the heights of heroism that she would reach. When her test came, she was ready. She had prepared herself with the Bread of Life.

One day Alessandro Serenelli, a youth whose family shared the same farmhouse with the Goretti's, whispered something appalling in Maria's ear. He wanted Maria to commit a terrible sin. The child could hardly believe what she heard. Maria's reply was emphatic: "No! No! It is a sin! I will not commit a sin!" Alessandro, however, persisted, pestering her constantly. The budding saint's response never varied: "No! No! It is a sin!" With a saint's wisdom, she avoided her tormentor. Lust, however, held Alessandro captive. Come what might, he decided that he would have his way with young Maria.

One afternoon, his opportunity came. The Goretti family had gone to the fields. Maria was home doing her chores, alone. The afternoon silence was broken by the sound of Alessandro entering the room. Maria saw the danger. Terrified, she grew cold with fear. She was trapped! "Now," Alessandro demanded! Frantically, Maria tried to escape. Flashing a knife, the crazed Alessandro gave the child a horrifying ultimatum: "Give in or I will kill you!"

The Saint's Response

This was the frightening choice that faced our young heroine. With the grace received from Our Eucharistic Lord, she courageously said: "No! I will not! It is a sin. God forbids it." Enraged, the young man plunged the knife into Maria's body fourteen times. She fell to the floor, dying.

Several hours later, her horrified parents found her in a pool of blood. At first Maria refused to identify her assailant. Finally, at her mother's insistence, she said: "It was Alessandro, Mama. He wanted me to do a terrible thing. But, I did not want to commit a sin." This was the secret of Maria's martyrdom: "*I DID NOT WANT TO COMMIT A SIN.*"

Under these circumstances, Maria's responsibility would have been little, if any. However, the saints always put God first. Remember St. Dominic Savio's motto: "Death rather than sin!" Maria chose death rather than compromise God's will in the slightest. Maria Goretti's response is the response of the Catholic Church to the lust of the pagan world. *"NO! NO! IT IS A SIN!"*

The Model For Youth Of All Ages

The doctors at the hospital performed a painful operation with no anesthesia. It was useless. Our young saint was dying. A priest was summoned and she made her last confession. Maria then received Jesus in Holy Viaticum. The Eucharistic Lord Who had readied Maria for her hour of trial now prepared her for her passage to Heaven.

Before death came, one more act of heroism came from the heart of the young martyr. United with her Divine Friend in Holy Viaticum, she taught us another lesson in being His disciple. She said: "Mama! I forgive Alessandro. I pray that one day he will be with me in Heaven." With those words, Maria Goretti died.

Young people desperately need role models. St. Maria Goretti is an outstanding model! She always put God first! She chose death rather than jeopardize her purity. For the love of Jesus Christ, she said "No" at the cost of her life! Maria's love of the Lord was not limited to mere words. She proved it!

On June 24, 1950, Pope Pius XII bestowed upon Maria Goretti the highest honor possible. Referring to her as "the sweet little martyr of purity," the Pope proclaimed Maria to be a canonized saint of the Catholic Church. He named her the Patroness of Youth. St. Maria Goretti is the role model that God wants people of all ages to imitate, especially youth.

In the opening prayer of St. Maria's Mass, the Church prays: "Father, source of innocence and lover of chastity, you gave St. Maria Goretti the privilege of offering her life in witness to Christ. As you gave her the crown of martyrdom, let her prayers keep us faithful to your teaching."

The temptations tormenting today's youth can be conquered only by the power of Jesus Christ and the intercession of Our Blessed Mother. The frequent reception of the Sacraments of Penance and Holy Communion are indispensable channels of grace. St. Maria's strength of character came from Jesus Christ in the Blessed Sacrament.

Today's youth can be spared from the perils of paganism by developing a deep devotion to Jesus Christ in the Blessed Sacrament. Jesus Christ in the Holy Eucharist is the answer through the saving mystery of the Church. Youth must be nourished through the Holy Sacrifice of the Mass and by frequenting the Sacraments of Confession and Communion. Parents must teach their children to live sacramental lives, as did young Maria. St. Maria Goretti, Patroness of Youth, pray for us. Amen!

MARY! THE CHURCH'S FIRST TABERNACLE!

Immediately after the Annunciation, "Mary set out with haste into the hill country to a town of Judea, where she entered Zechariah's house and greeted Elizabeth" (Luke 1:39-40). St. Luke then describes the exchange of greetings between Our Blessed Mother and St. Elizabeth, concluding with Mary's Magnificat. He completes the episode with a short observation, the significance of which may escape our attention. "Mary remained with Elizabeth about three months before returning home." Can we not reflect from this account that the home of Zechariah and Elizabeth became the first church of Christendom? Mary was it's tabernacle because Jesus, the Son of God, was within her. She adored Him. Zechariah, Elizabeth and John the Baptist joined Mary in adoration of the Divine Savior.

Jesus Christ loves His Church. It is His Mystical Body. St. Paul says: "He delivered Himself up for her to make her holy, purifying her by the bath of water in the power of the word, to present to Himself a glorious Church, holy and immaculate, without stain or wrinkle of any kind" (Ephesians 5:25-27). The Second Vatican Council teaches that Our Blessed Lord summons every member of His Church to become a saint (see *Lumen Gentium*, N. 39-42).

The Catholic Church continues Our Lord's mission of the salvation and sanctification of souls until His Second Coming. Until "He comes again in glory," the priests of the Church make Jesus present in sacrifice and sacrament. These are the means needed in order for Christ's faithful to attain the salvation and the sanctification of their souls. The Council also teaches us that the Holy Eucharist is the "source and the summit of all the sacraments." Jesus said: "Let me solemnly assure you, if you do not eat the flesh of the Son of Man and drink his blood, you will have no life in you" (John 6:52).

Mary Is "The Church In Its Perfection"

August 15 is the Solemnity of the Assumption of the Blessed Virgin Mary into Heaven. The Mass formulary contains a wealth of teachings designed to inspire all to become "holy and immaculate, without stain or wrinkle of any kind." The Church reminds us that true Marian devotion leads the faithful to imitate Mary in the practice of virtue.

Drawing from the richness of the Second Vatican Council, the Preface of the Mass prays: "The Virgin Mother of God was taken up into Heaven to be the beginning and the pattern of the Church in its perfection, and a sign of hope and comfort for your people on their pilgrim way."

The Universal Call to Holiness, a key teaching of Vatican II, emphasizes Our Lord's mandate: "Be ye perfect as your Heavenly Father is perfect" (Matthew 5:48). The Blessed Virgin Mary, who has already gained this perfection, must be our model. The Council teaches: "While in the most holy Virgin, the Church has already reached that perfection whereby she is without spot or wrinkle, the followers of Christ still strive to increase in holiness by conquering sin" (*Lumen Gentium*, N. 65).

Mary is the image and model of the Church in its perfection. She is the perfect pattern of the person God expects all followers of Jesus to become. Mary is the Virgin Most Humble, the Virgin Most Obedient, the Virgin Most Pure. She attained the heights of charity and patience, practicing all of the virtues perfectly. Appropriate are Wordsworth's words: "Woman! Above all women glorified; our tainted nature's solitary boast; purer than foam on central ocean tost!"

"In Consideration Of The Merits Of Jesus"

Pope Pius IX, in defining the dogma of the Immaculate Conception, proclaimed that: "The Blessed

Virgin Mary, by a unique grace and privilege of the omnipotent God, and *in consideration of the merits of Jesus*, the Savior of the human race, was preserved free from all stain of original sin" (*Ineffabilis Deus*, 1854).

This means that, although Our Blessed Mother was immaculately conceived, she also was redeemed by Jesus Christ. According to Blessed John Duns Scotus, Our Lady's redemption was preventive in that she was preserved free from Original Sin. Our redemption was curative in that we were cleansed from our sins. Thus, Blessed Scotus, who is known as the "Subtle Doctor," claims that Mary's redemption was more radical than our own. She was redeemed in a more sublime way.

The Virgin Mary Is The New Eve

Mary lived her life in total obedience to the Mosaic Law. She achieved the high degree of holiness that it mandated to the fullest. With joyful hope, Mary awaited the coming of the promised Redeemer.

In the "fullness of time," God sent His messenger to her. In the eternal plan of the Father, she was to be the new Eve. When Gabriel announced to Mary that she was chosen to be the mother of the Messiah, she said: "Behold the handmaid of the Lord. Be it done unto me according to thy word" (Luke 1:38). The first Eve responded to the temptation of a fallen angel in pride and disobedience. She wanted to be "like God."

Mary, the new Eve, responded to the announcement of the Archangel Gabriel in humility and obedience. "YES!" She would do God's will; she is the "handmaid" of the Lord. For the first time in the history of man's creation, the Father was completely pleased with one of His children. At the moment of her "*Fiat*," she conceived of the Holy Spirit. The Eternal Word of God became Flesh in her womb. Her Son is the New Adam, Jesus Christ, the Redeemer of Man.

The Three Days' Loss

At the moment of Christ's conception, Mary became the Church's first tabernacle. The Divine Presence of Jesus Christ sanctified her in a sublime way. Our Blessed Mother was with Jesus at every moment. There was only one exception. It happened when Jesus was a boy of twelve.

The Holy Family had gone to Jerusalem for the Feast of the Passover. "As they were returning at the end of the feast, the Child Jesus remained behind, unknown to His parents" (Luke 2:44). This three-day loss was one of the most bitter of Mary's Seven Dolors.

For three days, Mary had lost Jesus. She did not know where He was. It was an agony that only St. Joseph could understand. His anguish was almost as intense as hers for he was entrusted by God to be the Protector of the Holy Family. Joseph too had lost the Presence of Jesus for the first time. Perhaps we may have a tiny glimpse of what Mary and Joseph experienced when we enter a Catholic Church on Good Friday. The church is not the same. The tabernacle is empty. Jesus is gone.

Can we not see from these considerations that without Our Lord, truly Present in the Eucharist, it is impossible to achieve the sanctity to which we are called? Through the Eucharistic Presence of Jesus in sacrifice and sacrament, we receive the indispensable graces that we must have for our salvation and sanctification.

The liturgy also teaches us that Mary, gloriously assumed into Heaven, is "a sign of hope and comfort for your people on their pilgrim way." Mary, our mother and our model, intercedes for us in Heaven. Like every good mother, she longs for our safe arrival "home." We are a redeemed people, St. Paul says, destined for "citizenship in Heaven" (Philippians 3:20).

"Death Is Swallowed Up In Victory!"

The Second Reading of the Vigil Mass of the Assumption exuberantly exclaims: "Death is swallowed up in victory. O death, where is your victory? O death, where is your sting? The sting of death is sin, and sin gets its power from the law. But thanks be to God who has given us victory through our Lord Jesus Christ" (1 Corinthians 15:55-57).

By His redemptive death on the Cross of Calvary, Our Divine Savior has achieved complete victory over sin, Satan and death. Jesus rose precisely because He had overcome death. On the Solemnity of the Assumption of the Virgin Mary into Heaven, the Church, gathered around Christ Our King, honors the Holy Mother of God. How wonderful it is that we also can call her, Our Blessed Mother!

Reflecting on the glorious Assumption of Our Blessed Mother into heaven, let us join the angels and the saints in Heaven, the souls in purgatory, and the Church on earth in singing out: "All honor to you, Mary! Today you were raised above the choirs of angels to lasting glory with Christ" (Entrance Antiphon, Mass of the Assumption). Amen!

A LACK OF REVERENCE CANNOT BE SEPARATED
FROM A LACK OF PIETY!

It is often said: "Once an altar boy, always an altar boy." Having served at the altar of God, I believe this to be quite true. I have fond memories of my days as an altar boy. What a privilege it was to assist at the altar of God as the priest offers the Holy Sacrifice of the Mass.

Several years ago, I attended an annual Altar Boy's Mass which was offered at the Cathedral of a large eastern diocese. About five hundred boys from various parishes were present. Although difficult to manage at times, the boys were generally well behaved. Robed in their cassocks and surplices, they were an impressive group.

When it was time for Holy Communion, the boys processed to the altar. One young man in particular caught my attention. He was chewing gum! When he reached the priest, he spit the gum onto his left hand and reached out for the Sacred Host with his right. After casually popping the Body of Christ in his mouth, he placed the chewing gum on top. He continued chewing on his way back to the pew. Obviously, he was completely oblivious of his irreverent behavior.

Those of us from another era gasp in disbelief when we see such things. What have we taught our young people? Has modern society become so boorish that it even has lost respect for the Divine Presence? Yes! Jesus objected to false public displays of devotion (see Matthew 23:1-12). Yet, there are certain rules of comportment that must guide our attitude toward the Eucharist and our conduct in God's house. One's exterior manner often reveals one's interior disposition. Exterior manners can also influence interior dispositions.

Bishop Robert Carlson of Sioux Falls, South Dakota, gently admonishes his flock concerning this matter:

"Do we keep a prayerful attitude before, during and after Mass in the church? Surely, chewing gum in church before receiving Holy Communion does not give good example to our youth and must be avoided" (Pastoral Letter, "The Pledge of Future Glory," June 18, 1995).

"To Help Deepen Your Knowledge"

The Diocese of Lincoln, Nebraska conducted a Eucharistic Congress in 1995. They compiled a marvelous booklet entitled: *The Little Catechism on the Holy Eucharist*. Its purpose is clear. "(The Little Catechism) is offered to help you deepen your knowledge of, and love for, the Eucharist. This booklet contains a brief explanation of what Catholics believe about the Eucharist." The Little Catechism also offers an excellent "selection of prayers devoted to the Eucharist."

Concerning the Holy Sacrifice of the Mass, it succinctly presents Church teachings. "Even though the Sacrifice of the Cross that Jesus offered on Calvary for our salvation happened a long time ago in a far away place, it becomes present here and now at every Mass. Our Mass is the exact Sacrifice that Jesus offered on Calvary" (page 12).

Respect For The Eucharist

In these meditations on the Holy Eucharist, I have attempted to present the basic requirements for the worthy reception of Holy Communion. The Little Catechism makes this important observation: "We must not eat or drink anything except water and medicine, for one hour before receiving Holy Communion (this includes such things as chewing gum, coffee, tea, pop and candy)" (page 17).

Perhaps some may dismiss this admonition as a triviality. Nevertheless, it is clear that the consumption of these foods breaks the Eucharistic fast. Sad to say, the practice of chewing gum in church has become commonplace.

Chewing gum in church is simply inconsistent with respect for the Divine Presence. It displays a cavalier attitude toward the sacred.

Would a reasonable person chew gum or smoke in the presence of a prestigious person? Of course not! Yet, the Son of God is truly Present in our tabernacles! Centuries ago, St. Thomas More asked: "If you are brought into the presence of the prince, do you speak to him casually . . . then yawn, stretch or belch without giving it a thought? Would you conduct yourself in such a way as to give the impression that while you are addressing him you are thinking about something else?" (See *The Sadness of Christ,* by St. Thomas More.)

Talking And Immodesty In Church

Many Catholics are appalled by the loud talk and laughter that are now commonplace in Catholic churches. The Little Catechism offers this rule: "Only talk in church when we have to, like singing and saying the prayers at Mass, or in order to be polite to someone who asks us a question, but answer in a quiet voice" (page 32).

Equally disturbing is disrespectful dress in church. Some men and women attend Mass wearing shorts and other casual forms of attire. It is not unusual to see women in revealing and often provocative attire. This is entirely inappropriate. Modesty in dress is a requirement of Christian modesty in all public places, especially in church.

The *Catechism of the Catholic Church* lists modesty as one of the twelve fruits of the Holy Spirit (N. 1832). Clearly, it teaches that: "Purity requires modesty, an integral part of temperance" (N. 2521). Moreover, it makes this common-sense observation: "Modesty is decency. It inspires one's choice of clothing. It keeps silence or reserve where there is evident risk of unhealthy curiosity. It is discreet" (N. 2522).

The Little Catechism on the Holy Eucharist makes this exhortation: "Dress properly remembering that we are going into God's house. Jesus does care how we dress, because the clothes we pick out to wear shows what we think about the person or place we are going to visit" (Little Catechism, page 32).

Bishop James C. Timlin of Scranton, PA, recently addressed this lack of reverence in a letter written to the priests of his diocese. He said: "We can talk until we are blue in the face and with all theological precision about the Real Presence of Christ in the Blessed Sacrament but the fact is that conduct before this mystery has the power either to establish in the minds and hearts of our listeners the truth that we teach, or it has the power to undo that same truth."

Bishop Timlin insists that: "Generally, the absence of the acts of reverence I am speaking of consists in:

1) Failing to genuflect when entering or leaving church where in the Blessed Sacrament is reserved in the Tabernacle or failing to genuflect when passing before the Tabernacle;
2) Speaking or conversing in the presence of the reserved Sacrament as if one were not in a sacred place;
3) Failing to dress properly for church: e.g., beach attire is not appropriate in church."

Centuries ago, the Council of Trent summed up quite well the question of proper attitudes in Church, especially during Holy Mass. Irreverence, the Council taught, can scarcely be separated from ungodliness or superstition, a false imitation of true piety (Session 22, Chapter 9, On the Mass).

In regard to a proper attitude before the Blessed Sacrament, His Eminence, Cardinal Stickler teaches us that: "The Council of Trent has already pointed out that the lack of awe corresponds to a lack of piety and even more: a positive irreverence corresponds to a real impiety."

The Manner Of Reception

In many countries, the Church has granted permission for the reception of Holy Communion in the hand. When one chooses to receive in this manner, the proper method of reception must be observed. One must place the right hand under the left, forming with one's hands a throne for Our Blessed Lord. After the minister places the Body of Christ on the hand, the recipient reverently takes the Host in his right hand, says "Amen," and then immediately consumes the Sacred Species.

As is obvious to all, abuses abound. Often, they are the result of the thoughtlessness or ignorance on the part of well-intentioned persons. Some people, for example, reach out one hand and then pop the Host in their mouths. Others will take the Blessed Sacrament half way down the aisle or back to the pew before consumption. I once observed someone take the Host back to the pew and break it in half. When I confronted this person, the reply was: "I am having some now and saving the rest for lunch." Many other distressing examples can be cited.

Let us always remember that Jesus Christ is the Son of God. He is True God and True Man. We must worship Our Lord in His Divinity and in His Humanity. His presence in the Blessed Sacrament is not symbolic. It is the Real Presence! We must conduct ourselves accordingly. Being human, however, all of us must be reminded of these realities at times.

Perhaps the reverence of those who have gone before us can serve as a model. I remember my grandmother before she died. She could no longer attend Mass and was barely able to walk without her cane. Father Paul Brennan from the Annunciation Parish would bring her Holy Communion. Father told her that she did not have to kneel because of the difficulty that it presented for her. "No," she would say in her native Italian, "*in ginocchio.*" "I will kneel." Father and I helped her down on her knees. After she received Our Lord, we each took an arm as Grandmom struggled back to her chair. Yes! My grandmother could have received while sitting. But Maria Rego believed in the Real Presence and she showed it. She taught me a lesson in respect for the Blessed Sacrament that I will never forget. Our Blessed Lord saw her faith and I know that He will reward her for it.

May Mary, the Virgin Mother of God, protect us from the pagan influences of our times. May she teach us to love Jesus in the Blessed Sacrament and to display that love with a proper attitude of reverence and respect. Our Lady of the Most Blessed Sacrament, pray for us!

"THROUGH HIM, WITH HIM AND IN HIM"

Pope St. Pius X, revered as the Pontiff of the Eucharist, said: "Do not pray at Mass, but pray the Mass." Decades later, the Second Vatican Council taught that the faithful are not to attend the Holy Sacrifice as "strangers or silent spectators." The Council went on to teach: "The faithful should be instructed by God's word and nourished at the table of the Lord's Body. They should give thanks to God. By offering the Immaculate Victim, not only through the hands of the priest but also with him, they should learn to offer themselves. Through Christ the Mediator, they should be drawn day by day into ever more perfect union with God and with each other so that, finally, God may be all in all" (*Sacrosanctum Concilium*, N. 48). What does all this mean?

The Mass Is The Perfect Sacrifice

Jesus Christ, the Great High Priest, offered to the Heavenly Father the Sacrifice of Himself in expiation for the sins of the world. His Perfect Sacrifice of the Cross atoned for the sins of every person, from Adam to the last person who will walk the face of the earth. St. Paul says: "Jesus offered one sacrifice for sins and took his seat forever at the right hand of God; now he waits until his enemies are placed beneath his feet. By this one offering he has forever perfected those who are being sanctified" (Hebrews 10:14; see also 7:27,9:14,28).

In 1562 the Council of Trent dogmatically taught that every Mass is offered for four ends or purposes: Adoration, Thanksgiving, Propitiation and Petition. Responding to the Lutheran heresies that were then ravaging the Church, Trent used strong and precise language. "If anyone says that the Sacrifice of the Mass is only one of praise and thanksgiving; or that it is a mere commemoration of the Sacrifice consummated on the Cross but not a propitiatory one; or that it profits him only who receives, and ought not to be offered for the living and dead, for sins and punishments, satisfactions, and other necessities, let him be anathema" (Session 22, Canon 3).

Assisting at Mass, Christ's faithful offer their prayers in Adoration, Thanksgiving, Propitiation and Petition. United with the whole Mystical Body, the people do this through Christ, with Christ and in Christ. The Holy Sacrifice is the man's perfect way of achieving these four purposes.

Adoration

Every creature, both spiritual and material, must give glory to the Creator. The whole material universe, the sun, moon, stars, and planets give honor and glory to the Creator by their existence. The same is true of the vegetative and the animal kingdom. Man, made in the image and likeness of God, also must give Him honor and glory. Because of man's intelligence and free will, however, he is able to adore God freely.

The *Catechism of the Catholic Church* teaches: "The Eucharist is also the sacrifice of praise by which the Church sings the glory of God in the name of all creation. This sacrifice of praise is possible only through Christ: He unites the faithful to His Person, to His praise, and to His intercession, so that the sacrifice of praise to the Father is offered through Christ and with Him, to be accepted in Him" (N. 1361).

Thanksgiving

The word Eucharist itself comes from the Greek word meaning thanksgiving. In beautiful language, the Catechism stresses our need of giving thanks to God. "In the preface, the Church gives thanks to the Father, through

Christ, in the Holy Spirit for all His works: Creation, Redemption, and Sanctification. The whole community thus joins in the unending praise that the Church in Heaven, the angels and all the saints, sing to the thrice-holy God" (N. 1352). In union with Christ, the faithful offer perfect Thanksgiving.

Through Christ Our Lord, we thank God for His gift of Creation. He has given us the gift of life, the gift of Catholic Faith in the world in which we live. Everything that we have is God's gift, freely given (see 1 Corinthians 4:7). Therefore, we must render constant thanks to Almighty God (see Luke 17:11-19).

Through Christ, we thank the Father for the gift of Redemption. "Yes, God so loved the world that he gave His only begotten Son, so that whoever believes in him may not die but may have eternal life. God did not send the Son into the world to condemn the world, but that the world might be saved through him" (John 3:17). We read in the *Exsultet* of the Easter Vigil: "How precious must man be in the eyes of the Creator, if he gained so great a Redeemer."

Yes! God indeed loves us! He did not leave us in our sins. In justice, He could have condemned us because of our sins. But the Father, "who is rich in mercy," sent the Son to save us from sin, Satan and eternal death. Through Christ and His grace we strive for sanctification.

The Church prays in the preface of Eucharistic Prayer II: "For our sake (Jesus) opened His arms on the Cross; He put an end to death and revealed the Resurrection. In this He fulfilled Your Will and won for You a holy people."

St. Paul says: "God chose us in (Christ) before the world began to be holy and blameless in his sight, to be full of love" (Ephesians 1:4). In view of the magnitude of our sins, how can we ever attain holiness? Our voyage to salvation and sanctification must begin with the Mass and the

Sacraments, especially the Blessed Sacrament. These are the principal channels of grace.

Propitiation

Propitiation means that Mass is offered for the forgiveness of venial sins and the temporal punishment due for mortal sins already forgiven. The Catechism is clear that: "The Eucharist is not ordered to the forgiveness of mortal sins. That is proper to the Sacrament of Reconciliation" (N. 1395).

Yet, in a world drenched with sin, the Holy Sacrifice of the Mass makes mercy possible. Modern man's litany of sins seems overwhelming: the tremendous sins against faith, indifference and often open hostility to Almighty God, the blasphemies and desecrations of the Eucharist, the untold millions of abortions and other sins against human life. The list seems endlessly long!

The Seven Capital Sins abound: Pride, Covetousness, Lust, Anger, Gluttony, Envy, and Sloth. Sad to say, modern society and the mass media often glamorize these offenses against God. Pope John Paul II commented on this in his encyclical *Evangelium Vitae*: "When conscience calls 'evil good and good evil' (Isaiah 5:20), (society) is already on the path to the most alarming corruption and the darkness of moral blindness" (N. 24). Because of the infinite merits of the Mass, God withholds His just punishments.

Notice that the Church prays for the faithful departed at every Mass. United with Christ, we offer propitiation for the sins of the living and the dead. Catholics always have prayed for all the faithful departed. However, we often witness at present day funeral Masses "instant canonizations." This is a grave disservice to the deceased person. We simply do not know when a soul goes to heaven. The deceased person might be in Purgatory and in need of our prayers. Let us never neglect to pray for the souls in Purgatory.

St. Monica's dying words to her sons, St. Augustine and his brother, were: "Put this body anywhere! Don't trouble yourselves about it! I simply ask you to remember me at the Lord's altar wherever you are" (see *Catechism*, N. 1371).

Petition

"In the intercessions, the Church indicates that the Eucharist is celebrated in communion with the whole Church in Heaven and on earth, the living and the dead, and in communion with the pastors of the church, the Pope, the diocesan bishop, his presbyterium and his deacons, and all the bishops of the whole world together with their churches" (*Catechism*, N. 1354).

Devotion to Our Blessed Mother is thus of paramount importance. She, along with the whole heavenly court, is with us at every Mass. We on earth must follow her guidance and example. The Second Vatican Council teaches: "While in the most Holy Virgin the Church has already reached that perfection whereby she is without spot or wrinkle, the followers of Christ still strive to increase in holiness by conquering sin. And so they turn their eyes to Mary who shines forth to the whole community of the elect as the model of virtues" (*Lumen Gentium*, N. 65).

It is evident that our petitions at Mass, both public and private, are not made alone. United with Christ's Mystical Body, in heaven, purgatory and on earth, we present our needs to the Triune God. Our petitions culminate in the Our Father, the prayer that Jesus taught us.

At the end of the Eucharistic Prayer, the priest lifts the chalice and the paten. He prays: "Through Him, with Him and in Him, in the unity of the Holy Spirit, all honor and glory is Yours, Almighty Father, forever and ever." The assembly responds: "Amen!" We have said "Yes" to Adoration, Thanksgiving (especially for Redemption), Propitiation and Petition.

Christ's faithful then kneel and await the "Sacred Banquet," the Body and Blood of Our Divine Savior. Jesus Christ is the Lamb of God who takes away the sins of the world. Like St. Thomas the Apostle, we adore Our Blessed Lord by exclaiming: "My Lord and my God!"

THE EUCHARIST AS HOLY VIATICUM

There is a marvelous section in the *Catechism of the Catholic Church* dealing with the Anointing of the Sick and Holy Viaticum (N. 1499-1525). It contains vital information about "the sacraments that prepare us for our heavenly homeland." Having been "baptized into Christ Jesus," we want to do all that is possible to insure that we make our last journey "in Christ Jesus." The Holy Roman Catholic Church shows us the way.

The Anointing Of The Sick

The Church's Sacred Tradition confirms Extreme Unction as one of the seven sacraments instituted by Christ. Although St. Mark alluded to it (6:13), it was the Apostle James who promulgated it (5:14-15).

Whom can the priest anoint? In the year 1551, the Council of Trent taught that "this anointing is to be given to the sick, especially those who are in such a serious condition as to appear to have reached the end of their lives" (Session 14, Chapter 3).

The Second Vatican Council added: "Extreme Unction, which may also and more properly be called 'Anointing of the Sick,' is not a sacrament only for those who are at the point of death. Hence, as soon as any of the faithful begins to be in danger of death from sickness or old age, the fitting time for that sacrament has already arrived" (*Constitution on the Liturgy*, N. 73).

The Code of Canon Law mandates: "The Anointing of the Sick can be administered to any member of the faithful who, having reached the age of reason, begins to be in danger of death by reason of illness or old age. This sacrament can be repeated if the sick person, having recovered, again becomes seriously ill or if, in the same illness, the danger becomes more serious" (N. 1004).

The General Instruction of the Pastoral Care of the Sick directs that a person need not be "gravely ill," but should be "seriously ill." It also allows for persons to be "anointed before surgery whenever a serious illness is the reason for the surgery." The Instruction grants priests wide prudential discretion in the sacrament's administration. Faithful to the Church's teaching, however, it warns that Anointing "may not be given indiscriminately or to any persons whose health is not seriously impaired."

Effects Of Anointing Of The Sick

Pope Paul VI, in the Apostolic Constitution on the *Sacrament of the Anointing of the Sick*, lists four effects of the sacrament:

1) It takes away sins and the remnants of sin (that is, all of the temporal punishment due to sin).
2) It strengthens the sick person's soul and arouses confidence in God's mercy, giving him the strength to bear sufferings patiently.
3) It gives strength to resist the temptations of the devil who makes his last assault on the dying person's soul.
4) It sometimes restores bodily health "if this is expedient for the health of the soul" (See Council of Trent; *Catechism*, N. 1520).

The Sacrament Of Penance

Although the Sacrament of Anointing takes away the remnants of sin and the temporal punishment due to sin, one must be properly disposed to receive it (see *Summa*, Suppl. Q.30, A.1) The Second Vatican Council, faithful to Tradition, mandates that when possible "the sick man is anointed after he has made his confession and before he receives Viaticum" (*Sacrosanctum Concilium*, N. 74). The sick person finds the presence of the Merciful Savior in the priest who forgives sin "acting in the Person of Jesus Christ." Unfailingly, the words of absolution bring peace and comfort to the afflicted person.

If one is a proper candidate for anointing, especially when there is the danger of death, never delay the reception of the sacraments. If possible, *do not wait until the person has already died before sending for a priest.* Delay may deprive the person of crucial sacramental graces. The Instruction stresses that everything should be done to make possible the "active participation" of the sick person.

We must never delay the Sacrament of Anointing until the sick person is at the very doors of death. St. Robert Bellarmine tells us that the early Christians, hoping for bodily health for the sick person from the holy anointing, did not delay this sacrament until the doctors saw no hope of recovery. "The second kind of remains of sin is a sort of horror and torpor, or sadness and grief which comes over the sick. And to this the promise of St. James refers, 'And the Lord will raise him up' (James 5:15). For this sacrament cheers up the sick when they see the divine promises which are expressed in this venerable sacrament. And for this reason it should not be postponed until the last moment when the sick person hears and understands nothing" (*The Art of Dying*, Book 2, Chapter 8).

Holy Viaticum

The *Catechism of the Catholic Church* further teaches: "Just as the sacraments of Baptism, Confirmation and the Eucharist form a unity called 'the sacraments of Christian initiation,' so too it can be said that Penance, the Anointing of the Sick and the Eucharist as Viaticum constitute, at the end of Christian life, 'the sacraments that prepare for our heavenly homeland' or the sacraments that complete the earthly pilgrimage" (N. 1525).

The Latin word *viaticum* means provisions for a journey. Our Lord in Holy Viaticum is the Divine Provision for our journey into eternity. To understand the Eucharist as Holy Viaticum, perhaps an analogy may be useful. On Calvary, a confirmed criminal was crucified with Our Blessed Lord. The desperate man looked into the Savior's eyes. He saw His patience, His goodness and His compassion. But more important, the thief saw in Jesus Christ a Priest. He saw the Lamb of God who takes away the sins of the world. Could we not also speculate that he looked down and saw Mary? Perhaps she looked his way and his eyes met the eyes of the Mother of Mercy. Is she not the Refuge of Sinners and the Gate of Heaven?

Responding to grace, the repentant rogue pleaded: "Lord! Remember me when you come into your kingdom." The Great High Priest was swift in absolution: "I assure you: this day you will be with me in Paradise" (Luke 23:39-43). The Good Thief entered Heaven in the embrace of Jesus Christ.

In a sense, this is what happens when the Church comes to the dying person with her sacraments. In the Sacraments of Penance and Anointing, the dying Christian receives the forgiveness of sin and all its temporal punishments. Grace to resist the last onslaught of the Devil flows in abundance.

Having been "baptized into Christ Jesus," the dying person now receives Our Lord in Holy Viaticum. The Merciful Jesus gives the same assurance that He gave the Good Thief. Our Savior, united with the dying person in Holy Viaticum, personally accompanies his or her soul into eternal bliss.

In the Document on the *Life and Ministry of Priests*, Vatican II teaches: "All of the sacraments, as well as every ministry of the Church and work of the apostolate, are tied to the Eucharist and are directed toward it" (N. 5). As Our

Lord Jesus accompanies us on our earthly journey in Holy Communion, He escorts us on our last journey in Holy Viaticum.

Jesus, Mary and Joseph, I give you my heart and my soul. Jesus, Mary and Joseph, assist me in my last agony. Jesus, Mary and Joseph, may I breathe forth my last breath in union with You.

May the Heart of Jesus, in the Most Blessed Sacrament, be praised adored and loved, with grateful affection, in all the tabernacles of the world, even to the end of time. Amen!

PRAYERS

Act of Consecration to
the Most Sacred Heart of Jesus

O most loving Jesus, Redeemer of the human race, behold us humbly prostrate before Your altar. We are Yours and Yours we wish to be. But to be more surely united to You, behold each one of us freely consecrates himself today to Your most Sacred Heart. Many, indeed, have never known You; many, too despising Your precepts, have rejected You. Have mercy on them all, most merciful Jesus, and draw them to Your Sacred Heart.

Be King, O Lord, not only of the faithful who have never forsaken You, but also of the prodigal children who have abandoned You. Grant that they may quickly return to their Father's house, lest they die of wretchedness and hunger.

Grant, O Lord, to Your Church, assurance of freedom and immunity from harm. Give peace and order to all nations. Make the earth resound from pole to pole with one cry: Praised to the Divine Heart of Jesus that wrought our salvation. To It be glory and honor forever. Amen.

A Private Act of Reparation

Lord, see us kneeling before You. See us drawn to Your Heart, aware of our weakness and Your strength, our indifference and Your steadfast love, our coldness and Your everlasting warmth. By this homage we pay You, let us make up for all the failures to love, all the insults we pay You, all the neglect and carelessness. Accept the offering of our lives to make up for the wounds You have received from unbelievers, traitors and willful sinners. We offer this reparation through Your Sacred Heart, pierced for all men and raised up in triumphant glory. Amen.

Prayer for the Souls in Purgatory

O gentle Heart of Jesus, ever present in the Blessed Sacrament, ever consumed with burning love for the poor captive souls in Purgatory, have mercy on them. Be not severe in Your judgments, but let some drops of Your Precious Blood fall upon the devouring flames. And, Merciful Savior, send Your angels to conduct them to a place of refreshment, light and peace. Amen.

Prayer in Time of Suffering

Behold me, my beloved Jesus, weighed down under the burden of my trials and sufferings, I cast myself at Your feet, that You may renew my strength and my courage, while I rest here in Your presence. Permit me to lay down my cross in Your Sacred Heart, for only Your infinite goodness can sustain me; only Your love can help me bear my cross; only Your powerful hand can lighten its weight. O Divine King, Jesus, whose heart is so compassionate to the afflicted, I wish to live in You; suffer and die in You. During my life be to me my model and my support. At the hour of my death, be my hope and my refuge. Amen.

Prayer Before Communion

Holy Father, receive me into Your tender paternity, to the end that having achieved the course in which I have commenced to run for love of You, I may receive You, my reward, as an eternal heritage. Most loving Jesus, receive me into Your loving fraternity. Bear with me the trials and heat of the day. Be my consolation in all my troubles, my companion and guide during the pilgrimage of this life. Holy Spirit, Love of God. Receive me into Your charity. Be the master, teacher and tender friend of my soul always. Amen.

Guardian Angel Prayer

Angel of God and guardian of my soul. You behold the face to face presence of the Most Holy Trinity. As a messenger of God, may I learn to obey your voice in my conscience, as you lead and guide me along the paths of life according to the holy will of God. May your inspirations fill my soul with the light of truth, and love for the Sacred Heart of Jesus in the Most Holy Eucharist, so that, one day, I may enjoy your companionship for all eternity in the Communion of the Saints, with Mary, the Queen of all the angels. Amen.

Personal Prayer

O most holy Heart of Jesus, fountain of every blessing, I adore You, I love You, and with a lively sorrow for my sins, I offer You this poor heart of mine. Make me humble, patient, pure and wholly obedient to Your will. Grant, good Jesus, that I may live in You and for You. Protect me in the midst of danger, comfort me in my afflictions, give me health of body, assistance in my temporal needs, Your blessing on all that I do, and the grace of a holy death. Amen.

Prayer to the Sacred Heart

O Most Sacred Heart of Jesus, pour down Your blessings abundantly upon Your holy Church, upon our Holy Father the Pope, and upon all the clergy; give perseverance to the just, convert sinners, enlighten unbelievers, bless our relatives, friends and benefactors, help the dying, free the souls in purgatory and extend over all hearts the sweet empire of Your love. Amen.

Fatima Prayer

O Most Holy Trinity, Father, Son and Holy Spirit, I adore You profoundly. I offer You the most Precious Body, Blood, Soul and divinity of Jesus Christ, present in all the tabernacles of the world, in reparation for the outrages, sacrileges and indifference by which He is offended. By the infinite merits of the Sacred Heart of Jesus and the Immaculate Heart of Mary, I beg the conversion of poor sinners. Amen.

Prayer of St. Thomas Aquinas

Almighty and everlasting God, behold I come to the Sacrament of Your only-begotten Son, our Lord Jesus Christ: I come as one infirm to the Physician of life, as one unclean to the fountain of mercy, as one blind to the light of everlasting brightness, as one poor and needy to the Lord of heaven and earth. Therefore I implore the abundance of Your measureless bounty that You would vouchsafe to heal my infirmity, wash my uncleanness, enlighten my blindness, enrich my poverty and clothe my nakedness, that I may receive the Bread of Angels, the King of kings, the Lord of lords, with such reverence and humility, with such sorrow and devotion, with such purity and faith, with such purpose and intention as may be profitable to my soul's salvation. Grant unto me, I pray, the grace of receiving not only the Sacrament of our Lord's Body and Blood, but also the grace and power of the Sacrament.

O most gracious God, grant me so to receive the Body of Your only-begotten Son, our Lord Jesus Christ, which He took from the Virgin Mary, as to merit to be incorporated into His mystical Body, and to be numbered among His members. O most loving Father, give me grace to behold forever Your beloved Son with unveiled face, whom now I purpose to receive veiled in the way. Amen.

Jesus in the Eucharist

O Jesus, humbled in the Eucharist to be the source and center of charity of the Catholic Church and the strength of souls, we offer Thee our prayers, our actions, our sufferings in behalf of Thy priests, to the end that each day may behold the wider extension of the Kingdom of Thy Sacred Heart. Amen.

Soul of Christ

Soul of Christ, sanctify me;
Body of Christ, save me.
Blood of Christ, inebriate me;
Water from the side of Christ, wash me.
Passion of Christ, strengthen me.
O good Jesus, hear me.
Within Your wounds, hide me;
Separated from You, let me never be;
From the evil one, protect me;
At the hour death, call me.
And close to You bid me, that with Your saints,
I may praise You forever and ever. Amen.

Prayer for Reconciliation

Almighty and everlasting God, who has appointed Your only-begotten Son to be the Redeemer of the world, and has been pleased to reconcile us through His Precious Blood, grant, we beseech You so to venerate and adore this price of our salvation, that Its power on earth may keep us from all things harmful, and its fruits bring us to the joys of heaven. Amen.

O Sacred Banquet

O sacred banquet in which Christ is received, the memory of His passion is renewed, the mind is filled with grace and a pledge of future glory is given to us. O Lord, You have given us bread from heaven: containing in itself all delight. O God, who under this wonderful Sacrament has left us a memorial of Your passion; grant us, we beseech You, so to venerate the sacred mysteries of Your Body and Blood, that we experience in ourselves the fruit of Your redemption. Amen.

Litany of the Blessed Virgin Mary
(The Litany of Loreto)

Lord, have mercy on us.
    Christ, have mercy on us.
Lord, have mercy on us. Christ hear us.
    Christ, graciously hear us.
God, the Father of Heaven,
    have mercy on us.
God, the Son, Redeemer of the world,
    have mercy on us.
God, the Holy Spirit,
    have mercy on us.
Holy Trinity One God,
    have mercy on us.

Holy Mary,
Holy Mother of God,
Holy Virgin of virgins,
Mother of Christ,
Mother of divine grace,
Mother most pure,
Mother most chaste,

pray for us.

Mother inviolate,
Mother undefiled,
Mother most amiable,
Mother most admirable,
Mother of good counsel,
Mother of our Creator,
Mother of our Savior,
Mother of the Church,
Virgin most prudent,
Virgin most venerable,
Virgin most renowned,
Virgin most powerful,
Virgin most merciful,
Virgin most faithful,
Mirror of justice,
Seat of wisdom,
Cause of our joy,
Spiritual vessel,
Vessel of honor,
Singular vessel of devotion,
Mystical rose,
Tower of David,
Tower of ivory,
House of gold,
Ark of the covenant,
Gate of heaven,
Morning star,
Health of the sick,
Refuge of sinners,
Comforter of the afflicted,
Help of Christians,
Queen of angels,
Queen of patriarchs,
Queen of prophets,
Queen of Apostles,

pray for us.

Queen of martyrs,
Queen of confessors,
Queen of virgins,
Queen of all saints,
Queen conceived without Original Sin,
Queen assumed into Heaven,
Queen of the most holy Rosary,
Queen of peace,

pray for us.

Lamb of God, Who takes away the sins of the world,
spare us, O Lord.
Lamb of God, Who takes away the sins of the world,
graciously hear us, O Lord.
Lamb of God, Who takes away the sins of the world,
have mercy on us.

V. Pray for us, O holy Mother of God,
R. That we may be made worthy of the promises of Christ.

Let us pray: grant we beseech Thee, O Lord God, that we Thy servants may enjoy perpetual health of mind and body, and by the glorious intercession of the Blessed Mary, ever Virgin, be delivered from present sorrow and enjoy everlasting happiness. Through Christ our Lord. Amen.

Illustrious Virgin

O most illustrious Virgin and Mother of our Lord Jesus Christ, who did worthily bear in thy sacred womb the very Creator of all things, whose most holy Body and Blood I have just received, vouchsafe to make intercession to Him in my behalf, that whatsoever I have omitted or committed in this unutterable Sacrament whether through ignorance, negligence or irreverence, may be graciously pardoned by thy dear Son in answer to thy most holy prayers. Amen.

Eucharistic Heart of Jesus

Eucharistic Heart of Jesus, I consecrate to Thee all the faculties of my soul, all the powers of my body, all the power of my being. I will strive to know Thee and love Thee ever more and more in order to make Thee better known and loved. I will act only for Thy glory and do all for the glory of Thy Father. I consecrate to Thee every moment of my life in a spirit of adoration before Thy Real Presence in a spirit of thanksgiving for this incomparable gift and in a spirit of reparation for all our indifferences. May our prayers, offered through Thee, with Thee and in Thee rise purified and enriched to the throne of God's mercy unto His eternal Glory and Thy Sacred and Eucharistic Heart. Amen.

Aspirations

Divine Heart of Jesus, convert sinners, save the dying, and deliver the holy souls in purgatory.

Heart of Jesus, burning with love for us, set our hearts on fire with love for Thee.

Jesus, meek and humble of heart, make our hearts like unto Thine.

O Sacrament most holy, O Sacrament divine! All praise and all thanksgiving be every moment Thine!

Love and honor and glory be to the Eucharistic Heart of Jesus!

Praise and adoration be ever more to Jesus in the most holy Sacrament of the Altar!

May the Eucharistic Heart of Jesus be praised and adored, loved and thanked at every moment in all the tabernacles of the world, unto the end of time.

Sacred Heart of Jesus, Thy Kingdom come!

GLOSSARY

The Altar

An altar is a table on which a sacrifice is offered. In a Catholic Church, the altar is the table on which the Holy Sacrifice of the Mass is offered. The altar is a symbol of Christ Who is offered. Traditionally, the main altar of a church has an altar stone that should be consecrated by a bishop. In it are relics of saints that reminds the faithful of their union with the entire Mystical Body of Christ.

Altar Bread

Altar bread is used in the Holy Sacrifice of the Mass. In order for the bread to become the Body of Christ, the altar bread must be true wheat bread. It became the custom in the Western church to use only unleavened bread in the Mass since it was the kind of bread that Jesus used at the Last Supper. Altar bread is baked in the form of a flat disk. The priest consecrates the altar bread during Mass and elevates a large Host.

Baptismal Font

A baptismal font is a basin used in the Sacrament of Baptism. The person being baptized has water poured over his head while the words of baptism are spoken. Baptismal fonts have been placed near the entrance of the church to show that Baptism is the door to Christ and His Church and the other sacraments.

Chalice

The chalice is a blessed cup, made of a metal of superior durability that is supported by a stem with a broad base at the bottom, used only at Mass for holding the Blood of Christ. The chalice should be nonporous since a material like wood would tend to become saturated with the Precious Blood.

The Confessional

The confessional is a place set aside in a church for the celebration of the Sacrament of Penance. In the early church, confessions were heard before the altar. In the sixteenth century, St. Charles Borromeo designed the confessional as it has been used since.

Ecumenical Council

The gathering of the bishops of the Catholic Church under the summons of the Holy Father to exercise their authority to declare, decree or define on matters pertaining to the faith, morals and discipline of the Church, subject to the final decision of the Supreme Pontiff.

Encyclical

A letter of the Holy Father concerning matters relating to the entire Church, usually sent to the bishops, that may pronounce on matters of faith and morals in which the teaching of Christ is restated or defined irrevocably.

Fasting

Fasting is the limiting of one's consumption of food and drink for a religious purpose. Traditionally, a fast day allowed for the eating of only a single meal. Currently, the Church allows for one main meal along with two lesser meals which do not equal the main meal. Fasting recognizes the need for dependence on God and is a means of reparation for sin. Catholics are obliged to fast on Ash Wednesday and Good Friday.

Grotto

A grotto is a cave or cavern. In Catholic tradition, it is a cave-like structure designed for the private prayer of the faithful. Most commonly, a grotto is built as a place for devotion to the Blessed Virgin Mary, since many of the approved apparitions of Mary have occurred in natural caves or grottos.

Holy Water

Holy water is water blessed for baptisms and used by the faithful as a reminder of their life in Christ. The term referred originally to the water blessed at the Easter Vigil. Holy water is usually placed near the entrance to churches where those entering can bless themselves with the Sign of the Cross, which recalls the baptismal commitment to be cleansed from sin through the grace of Christ.

Magisterium

The teaching authority of the Church divinely established by Christ that is vested in the bishops under the rule of the Holy Father, the apostolic successor of St. Peter. The bishops are given the authority to authentically teach what is divinely revealed by God.

Mystery

A divinely revealed truth that cannot be fully understood by the human mind. The mystery of God's revelation becomes intelligible to a believer through prayer, study and the grace of understanding.

Pyx

The pyx is a small sacred vessel with a lid that contains the Eucharist that is brought to the sick and the home bound. The pyx is generally made in a round, flat shape with a decorated lid and is normally carried in a case equipped with a cord that can be hung around the neck.

Relic

A relic can be a portion of the body, clothing or an article of a saint which may be placed in a reliquary or in an altar stone. The possession and veneration of relics is very ancient. A relic may be a small bone or even the complete body of a saint.

Sacrament

An outward sign instituted by Christ in which the graces merited by Christ on Calvary are applied to our souls. A sacrament signifies and confers divine grace. It is an act of Jesus that confers the grace it signifies.

Stations of the Cross

The Stations of the Cross are a series of fourteen images on the inside walls of a church commemorating the stages of Christ's journey to Calvary. In the early centuries, pilgrims to Jerusalem would travel the route of Jesus to Calvary, stopping along the way to meditate on the suffering of Christ. St. Francis of Assisi began the custom of setting up fourteen images representing the Way of the Cross.

Tradition

The passing on of God's revealed Word from one generation of the faithful to another under the guidance of the Church's authentic Magisterium inspired by the grace of the Holy Spirit.

Votive Candles

A votive candle, known also as a vigil light, is lit by the faithful to express a particular intention of prayer or to honor God and His saints. It symbolizes the ongoing prayer of the one who lit the candle.

Water and Wine

Water and wine are the elements mixed during the Mass that represent our humanity being united with the divinity of Jesus Christ. These elements are consecrated by the priest to become the Precious Blood of Christ in the Mass, which cleanses the faithful from their sins. The wine must be pure grape wine.

Additional materials by Father Rego

Booklets ----
A Contemporary Adult Guide to Conscience
  for the Sacrament of Confession   50 pages

The True Meaning of Love: The Beauty and
  the Wisdom of the Church's Teaching   51 pages

"No! No! It is a Sin!": A Message to the
  Young Adults of Today from Saint Maria
  Goretti, Patroness of Youth   70 pages

Audio Cassette ----
On the Mass and on Mary   40 min.

Audio Album (6 Cassette Mission Series) **----**
Jesus Christ, The Redeemer of Man   43 min.

The Mass: The Sacrifice and the Sacrament   45 min.

The Sacrament of Penance   50 min.

The Mystery of the Church   46 min.

The Papal Encyclical **Humanae Vitae**   49 min.

Mary, the Mother of the Church and
  our Blessed Mother   41 min.

The Leaflet Missal Company
976 W. Minnehaha Ave.
St. Paul, Mn 55104
Phone: (612) 487-2818
FAX: (612) 487-0286